DOES GOD LIKE BEING GOD?

DOES GOD LIKE BEING GOD?

And Other Tricky Questions about God

JOHN HONNER

A GUIDE FOR TEACHERS, CATECHISTS, AND PARENTS

Paulist Press
New York / Mahwah, NJ

Cover image by DasArts/Shutterstock.com
Cover and book design by Lynn Else

Library of Congress Cataloging-in-Publication Data
Names: Honner, John, author.
Title: Does God like being God? : tricky questions about God for teachers, catechists, and parents / John Honner.
Description: New York : Paulist Press, 2019.
Identifiers: LCCN 2018056320 | ISBN 9780809154371 (pbk. : alk. paper)
Subjects: LCSH: God (Christianity)—Miscellanea. | Catholic Church—Doctrines—Miscellanea.
Classification: LCC BT103 .H674 2019 | DDC 231—dc23 LC record available at https://lccn.loc.gov/2018056320

ISBN 978-0-8091-5437-1 (paperback)
ISBN 978-1-58768-832-4 (e-book)

Published by Paulist Press
997 Macarthur Boulevard
Mahwah, New Jersey 07430
www.paulistpress.com

Printed and bound in the
United States of America

For Samantha, Finn, and George

CONTENTS

CONTENTS

ACKNOWLEDGMENTS

"Why hasn't this been explained to us before?" This question has often been asked of me in the past few years, usually during intensive seminars with teachers and administrators who are undertaking degrees in theology, religious education, or ministerial leadership. Many of the chapters in this book have grown out of their discussions of the nature of faith and the tasks of theology. My thoughts would not have taken the shape of a book without their encouragement and provocation. I am therefore indebted to all those good people who concentrated my mind through courses at the University of Divinity, the Australian Catholic University, the University of Newcastle, and BBI–TAITE, the Australian Institute of Theological Education. I hope this book assists all teachers and leaders in their ministries.

My involvement with groups of lay sponsors of Catholic ministries has raised similar questions and discussions. Hopefully, this work will also be of service to them. I particularly thank my colleagues and friends in the governance and leadership of Mary Aikenhead Ministries, Edmund Rice Education Australia, and the Association of Ministerial Public Juridic Persons in Australia. They have challenged me to present theology in a way that is responsible, relevant, and accessible.

I thank the editors at Paulist Press for their insightful suggestions and warm encouragement. I am delighted to know that these experiences from Australia might be shared with a wider readership.

Finally, and most importantly, I thank everyone in my faith-filled and faith-challenging family. I thank you for your love and amusement and for all the conversations about faith and the meaning of life that we have shared. Hopefully, this book might offer guidance to parents everywhere who are trying to nurture their families in their relationship to God and help them to answer the questions their children ask them about God. It therefore seems appropriate to dedicate this book about God to Samantha, Finn, and George, my God-children from three Honner families. May they always be blessed.

INTRODUCTION

Why This Book?

This book is designed to help teachers, catechists, parents, and ministry leaders respond to the tricky and often highly intelligent questions that children and young people ask about God.

You can start reading this book wherever you wish, even starting with the tricky questions in part 2. While this book is written chiefly with a Catholic readership in mind, the questions are explored from the perspectives of Scripture, tradition, philosophy, and science and are intended for an inclusive rather than exclusive readership.

Tricky questions need large-minded answers. They stretch our contracting adult brains so that we might once again think with the open and agile minds of younger people. The great German Jesuit Karl Rahner described a child as "infinite openness to the infinite."[1] Good answers clarify mysteries without simplifying them. They keep us open to the infinite.

My first experience as a teacher of religious education was memorable. It was with a handful of youngsters on a Sunday morning in a tin shed beside a makeshift church in a newly developing suburb on the outskirts of Melbourne, Australia. It was a sunny, crisp autumn morning. A big man, whom I had never seen before, came up to me frowning and said, "If you teach my children that Adam and Eve didn't exist, then I'll drive my truck through your shed and flatten it." This was a warning shot from a father who was passionate about his faith and the way it would be passed on to his children.

Times have certainly changed. Today, the protests tend to come from the children. Michael McGirr, for example, a superb teacher of literature and religion, was

---

1. Karl Rahner, "Ideas for a Theology of Childhood," in *Theological Investigations*, vol. 8 (London: Darton, Longman & Todd, 1971), 33–50.

recently describing the experience of God to a class of adolescent boys. "Sir," interrupted one student, "do you know the meaning of the word *hallucination?*" There was much laughter. The questions young people ask about God today are sometimes oppositional, being influenced by the new atheists like Richard Dawkins and his *God Delusion*, but they also disclose a deep desire to know.

Teaching children and young people can be wonderful work because we are engaging with "infinite openness." Teaching Christian faith to young people gets complicated, however, because faith is ultimately an invitation into a personal relationship. All our descriptions of God can miss the mystery of the relationship and may lead to further tricky questions. Authentic teachers are usually given the benefit of the doubt and are not overly persecuted by their students. Honest teachers, nonetheless, wish they knew more about their subjects, particularly in teaching religion. This book aims to help teachers to understand more about God, to understand more about the reasonableness of faith, and to understand more about the ultimate incomprehensibility of God.

I know something of teachers' needs today because, after many years of lecturing in theology to candidates for ordination, I have, more recently, been working with teachers in Catholic schools. These women and men, for the most part, are school leaders and religious education coordinators. They are committed Christians, excellent leaders and teachers, and keen to understand their faith more deeply. They are also laity, asked to lead Catholic ministries, sometimes struggling to come to terms with the failures of the institutional Church. They are conscious of the gap between flourishing schools and struggling parishes. They have an innate sense of when Church authorities are authentic and when they are unconvincing, but they do not always understand why this is so or know how to take the next step, particularly when the issues are related to faith formation and Catholic education. This book is written for those who are nurturing the faith of the next generations of students and families, particularly parents.

In general, religious education, or "studies in religion," focuses on teaching students *about* various faiths and their key beliefs and practices. It sometimes moves into what is called "interfaith education." Special religious education, however, teaches students about their own faith—in as much as they or their families are aligned with a specific religion—and hopefully it also encourages them *in* their faith. Special religious education moves into the territory of "faith formation," helping students grow in both their relationship with God and in the practice and understanding of their faith. *Does God Like Being God: And Other Tricky Questions about God* is primarily concerned with faith formation: How do we help a young person hear how God is calling her? And how do we answer a young person's tricky questions?

We begin with four short chapters that lay the foundations for answering tricky questions: first, the simple basics of theology; second, that the Bible is our treasure; third, that faith is a personal relationship rather than doctrine; and finally, that some of the ways we express our faith can change. Subsequent chapters then focus on the tricky questions that students ask, questions like, "Who made God?" and "If God is almighty, why is there suffering?"

In reflecting on the tricky questions, we frequently draw on Scripture and Church teaching, as well as on science and philosophy. This traditional approach to theology may seem conservative and unimaginative, but rather, it is radical—going back to the roots. In chapter 4, we explain that the purpose of Church teaching is not about locking us into the past so much as about guiding us into the future.

Admittedly, there is not always a complete answer to the tricky questions that arise. Some questions about God are unanswerable, because God, by definition, is ultimately beyond our comprehension. Furthermore, the person asking the question is more important than the question itself. Often it is wiser to respond to the person than to the question. In other words, how we respond to tricky questions can vary from one person to another. We need to know if their question is a search to understand, a cry from the heart, or just oppositional behavior. Adolescents are experts in oppositional behavior, but that is only because they are trying to find their own identity and their own meaning. This is where talented teachers exercise their gifts.

I was once at a large religious education conference when a young teacher asked a question of a panel of experts about how she could authentically teach religion when her faith was so much less certain than her mother's faith, and how she struggled to accept some Church teachings and practices. How on earth, she asked, could she be a teacher of religion in a Catholic school? There was a general silence from the panel, of which I was a member. Perhaps none of us wanted to go down the wordy road of distinguishing one thing from another and laying out an intellectual response to what was also a cry from the heart. After we looked at each other in silence for a while, Professor M. Shawn Copeland from Boston College took the microphone and spoke in something like the following terms: "The first thing to say is that your mother raised a fine young Christian woman, giving her the spirit and wisdom and freedom to make her own good decisions on her faith journey...." I can't remember what followed, but this example of attending to the person before attending to the question has remained with me.

Consequently, in this book, I adopt simple language to explain elements of revelation, tradition, Church teaching, and theology that are relevant to the tricky questions that students continually ask, and we continually ask ourselves. Perhaps some of my reflections will not be age-appropriate responses to the questions that younger children may ask, but I hope they will help teachers have confidence in working out how to answer their questions truthfully.

Truth is important. Young people have a nose for truth. I have always been haunted by Yevtushenko's poem "Lies," which begins:

Telling lies to the young is wrong.
Proving to them that lies are true is wrong.
Telling them that God's in his heaven
and all's well with the world is wrong.
The young know what you mean. The young are
    people.
Tell them the difficulties can't be counted,
and let them see not only what will be
but see with clarity these present times.[2]

Hopefully, what follows will help us teach children the truth about God—who is not just in heaven—and about a living faith in these present times. May it also deepen your own faith and make your witness and understanding more effective in passing on the faith. Faith is a personal journey, and theology can be very simple.

Sometimes, we may not know the answers to every question about our faith. Nonetheless, the way we live and the way we teach will show students that we are true believers. As a student, I was inspired by a science teacher who, every morning on his way to his desk, made a quiet and unpretentious visit to the school chapel. Children may learn more from our example than we will ever know. A wise teacher once observed that our example will be the education our students will carry forward after they have forgotten everything else we taught them.

---

2. Yevgeny Yevtushenko, "Lies," in *Selected Poems*, trans. Robin Milner-Gulland and Peter Levi (London: Penguin, 2008), 52.

Part One

FOUNDATIONS OF
THEOLOGY

1

CAN THEOLOGY BE MADE SIMPLE?

Although often distracted by minute details, Christian theology is primarily concerned with helping the faith community address the difficult questions that arise from time to time. For example, in the very first days of the early Church, the first Christians asked such questions as, "Should Judas be replaced by another apostle?" (see Acts 1); "How can we care for the widows and orphans when we are so busy preaching?" (see Acts 6); and "Should gentile converts be circumcised?" (see Acts 15).

In response to each of these questions, we read that the community met together, discussed the issues, listened to various opinions and arguments, reflected on the Jewish Scriptures and the teachings of Jesus, noted the needs and concerns of the people, prayed to the Holy Spirit, and then came to an acceptable decision. Peter, recognized as leader of the community, often announced the final decision.

In the various letters of St. Paul, too, we see the growing and scattered Christian communities trying to understand the implications of their faith in these new circumstances: How to celebrate the Eucharist?; How to balance freedom and law?; How to continue to live in the world while waiting for resurrection?; How to overcome divisions?; and so on. St. Paul explained the faith to them, drawing on Scripture and his experience of Jesus. They came to understand their faith more deeply. They were doing what we call "theology": trying to understand issues that arose in living out their faith. They exemplified St. Anselm's classical definition of *theology* as "faith seeking understanding."

First, note that Christian theology happens from *within* the faith community, because the living faith is part of the data that theology considers. Theology in this respect is different from the academic discipline called the "Study of Religions." For example, if, as a Christian, you were to choose to study Islam, then you would be studying it as an outsider. You may be able to read the Qur'an, consider the history and practice of Islam, study the works of Islamic scholars, and so on, but you would not know what it is like to live the life of a faithful Muslim. You would be studying the religion from the *outside*, as an objective exercise.

A critic might say that theology, done from within the faith community, must then be *subjective* rather than *objective*. This is not quite accurate, however, because theology considers objective data—like the texts of Scripture or Church teaching—and a shared experience of faith. Ideally, therefore, theology is to be done not only in an academic setting, but also in the context of prayer and service. It needs to be sensitive to the dynamic presence of the Holy Spirit in the community. It has thus been said that we should do theology on our knees.

Second, following from the examples of the Acts of the Apostles, note that the work of a theologian is different from the work of the leader of the faith community. Theologians offer informed opinions, but sometimes they may disagree among themselves. The community of faith, listening to the arguments and guided by the Holy Spirit, discerns the way forward. For example, recalling Acts 15, some said that Gentile converts to Christianity should be circumcised because that was the Law of Moses, but this apparently strong argument was rejected: "After there had been much debate, Peter stood up and said to them....'God...testified to them [the Gentiles] by giving them the Holy Spirit, just as he did to us; and in cleansing their hearts by faith he has made no distinction between them and us'" (Acts 15:7–9).

The theologian, then, is a servant of the faith community, subject first to the movement of the Holy Spirit recorded in Scripture, second to the teaching office of the Church, and third to the sensitivity of the faithful who make up the Church.

Third, theology is an extreme science. Just as a theoretical physicist tries to understand and answer questions about the mysteries of the natural world, a Christian theologian tries to understand and answer questions about Christian faith and the mysteries of God. Scientific theory and Christian theology are separate but related ways of understanding ourselves and our world. *Theos*, the Greek word for a God who beholds all things, is possibly related to *theory*, the scientist's word for a way of beholding nature. A theologian is thus wise to heed the findings of science. This human thirst to know, from a Christian understanding, is a gift from God, an invitation into a relationship with God.

Since the early days of the Church, there have been synods and councils, creeds and controversies. There has been much Church teaching, much secular learning, and increasingly complicated social and political contexts. Theologians have emerged, skilled in learning and argument, to guide the community of the faithful into new times. Though they may have been controversial in their own time, many of them are now acknowledged as saints, such as Irenaeus, Athanasius, Augustine, Anselm, Thomas Aquinas, Bonaventure, and Peter Canisius, in past years, and Mary MacKillop, Dorothy Day, Mother Teresa, and Oscar Romero, in recent times.

Today, there are new questions of concern that disturb the community of the faithful—some great, some small: How can the Church be a poor Church for the poor?; Can non-Catholics be allowed to enroll in Catholic schools?; Can women be ordained to ministry?; Can divorced and remarried Catholics be allowed to receive holy communion?; Can laypeople be given positions of authority in the governance of the Church?; and so on.

How does a theologian shed light on these questions? By following these basic steps:

1. What light does Scripture shine on the question?
2. What light does the tradition of the Church (the early teachings) shine on the question?
3. What is the teaching of the Church regarding the question?
4. What are the needs and concerns of the people in the community of faith?
5. What can we discern of the movement of the Holy Spirit in the Church (the signs of the times)?
6. Are there any relevant findings in secular sciences that we should consider?
7. What new understanding emerges from all these factors?
8. How does the community of faith respond to our findings?

While this is a simple method, theologians, with their knowledge of minute details, can add much to the discussions. In answering the tricky questions in the following chapters, we will usually follow the formula above because this is not only a way of coming to understand the issues from the perspective of faith, but also a way of developing a habit for doing theology.

Whether we realize it or not, it is important to acknowledge that we each see theological issues through our own lens or framework. For example, each of our four Gospels looks at Jesus through a different lens and offers a different perspective on Jesus. This does not mean that they contradict each other, nor that one is truer than the others. Rather—and the Church shows inspired wisdom in including all four Gospels in its canon of Scripture—we need these different views of Jesus if we are to understand his identity and mission. For example, while there are some sharp contrasts between the Gospels of Mark and John—the former focused on the humanity and suffering of Jesus and the latter on the divinity and triumph of Jesus—we need both perspectives.

When we acknowledge the need to consider different perspectives on a question, then sometimes we can find a way of resolving the question. Many tricky questions just need a broader perspective. Sometimes both answers are right! It is often the case in theology that contradictory answers need to be held together. For example, God is believed to be both just and merciful, transcendent and immanent, and one and three. Jesus is described both as human and divine, as crucified and risen, and as fulfilling the Law and transcending the Law. Christians are both sinners and saved. The Bible is the Divine Word in human words.

While this combination of opposites might seem illogical and irrational, there are good arguments for using opposed complementary terms to provide a more complete description of reality. For example, in physics, we have the peculiar situation that an electron is understood as behaving as both a wave and a particle, even though waves are the opposite of particles.

A lot of tricky theological questions arise because we find it too mind-boggling to hold opposites together, and consequently, we get caught on one or the other of the horns of a dilemma. At this point, we may need to expand our imagination. Often the more profound theological answer is not "either...or" but "both...and." This can be difficult when young people often seek absolute clarity. Doing theology is like doing intellectual yoga: instead of stretching our muscles, we stretch our brains. The results, however, are greater mental agility and a freed-up intelligence.

One constant Christian theological dilemma is about whether we start theology "from above" or "from below." For example, as noted earlier, the Gospel of Mark focuses more on the humanity of Jesus and the suffering of the community. This is called a "low Christology" or a theology "from below." In John's Gospel, the focus is more on the divinity of Jesus, who became flesh and revealed the glory of God. This is called a "high Christology" or a theology "from above." If we only follow the path of theology from below, there is a risk that we will get caught up in the concerns of this world and lose sight of the divine. Jesus becomes a cool guy rather than an awesome transforming visionary. If we only follow the path of a theology from above, our focus may result in the worship of God to the neglect of the physical world of Jesus's incarnation. Either pathway alone is a dangerous simplification of Christian faith. In fact, if we read Mark and John carefully, we will see how they overlap in many ways.

It is also helpful to understand that the First Vatican Council (1869–70) occurred in the context of the decline of the Catholic Church as a political and intellectual authority in Europe. This happened for many reasons: the power of modern science, the rise of liberalism and democracy, and the collapse of the Holy Roman Empire. Vatican I thus focused on reestablishing the preeminence of the Church. Its most notable declarations were on the infallibility of the pope and the condemnation of modern rationalism and liberalism. The council asserted that where there was a clash between the findings of science and the judgments of faith, then science was to be rejected—clearly a theology "from above." Perhaps, if the council had not been prematurely closed by the entry of Italian soldiers into Rome, a more balanced theology might have emerged.

The Second Vatican Council (1963–65) offered a broader and more inclusive view of the Church and its place in the modern world. Its two key documents are about the relationship of the Church to the world: the Dogmatic Constitution on the Church (*Lumen Gentium*) and the Pastoral Constitution on the Church in the Modern World (*Gaudium et Spes*). The first document is about the light that Christ brings to the world through the Church. The second is about the needs of the world and how the Church is part of human society, rather than sitting above or separate from human society. The world is regarded as the theatre of God's activity.

As we work our way through some of the tricky questions in theology, it is useful to keep an eye on the theological starting points and frameworks that shape these questions, and the range of responses the Church offers. The best responses will be those that reflect on the whole of Scripture and the tradition of the Church and are alert to the movement of the Holy Spirit in and around the faith community. Vatican II thus describes the "task" of the theologian:

> The People of God believes that it is led by the Lord's Spirit, Who fills the earth. Motivated by this faith, it labors to decipher authentic signs of God's presence and purpose in the happenings, needs and desires in which this People has a part along with other men of our age. For faith throws a new light on everything, manifests God's design for man's total vocation, and thus directs the mind to solutions which are fully human. (*Gaudium et Spes* 11)

In conclusion, theology is simple in its intentions and methods, but it can be complicated in its details and explanations. Nevertheless, the key steps in theology remain clear: First, we ask ourselves, What does Scripture say? What does our tradition say? What does the Church teach? What do contemporary sciences say? Next, we reflect on the needs of the people and the movement of the Spirit. Then, we think and pray! As Vatican II states, "Sacred theology rests on the written word of God, together with sacred tradition, as its primary and perpetual foundation" (*Dei Verbum* 24).

Let us now briefly consider three related foundational topics: a theology of the Bible, a theology of faith, and a theology of Church teaching.

2

WHY IS THE BIBLE IMPORTANT?

Here is a test of what you value most: you have just received an emergency warning that a fast-moving wildfire is heading toward your house. You have ten minutes to gather your precious possessions and leave. What do you take with you? Jewelry? Personal papers like marriage certificates, passports, house titles, insurance contracts? Your laptop computer? Irreplaceable things like old photo albums, letters from your parents, family heirlooms? Wedding photos? The whole lot? Your daughter brings her custom-made skateboard, her diaries, and her favorite teddy called William. Your son gets his original Ramones T-shirt, his Gibson sunburst guitar, and his dog. The dog brings a ball. It's time to pack and run.

That's how the Bible got put together. Most of the Jewish Scriptures, as we read them now, were compiled in written form when the Jews were in exile in Babylon. There, like a family after a fire, they gathered together all the stories, poems, prayers, laws, customs, rituals, and revelations that were key to their identity after they had been driven out of Jerusalem. They remembered the patriarchs and prophets, the accounts of Creation, the stories of slavery in Egypt and escape to the promised land, God's covenant and commandments, the triumphs of David, extreme stories about characters like Job and Esther, Judith and Jonah, and details of the holy Law. History, song, poetry. There's even a story about a young man and his dog and an angel heading out on a journey to God: "The young man went out and the angel went with him; and the dog came out with him and went along with them" (Tob 6:1–2).

Some of these treasures may have been written down, but many older stories were passed on from one generation to the next as narratives, often with variations and changes of emphasis. When the Scriptures were being compiled, there may have been competing versions of the same stories. Choices had to be made. In hindsight, the people of God were deciding between what seemed true of God and what seemed false. In other words, they were discerning divine revelation. They gathered the events and stories that were truly awesome, revealing God and God's covenant.

Jesus was a Jew, and the Jewish Scriptures, sometimes called the Old Testament, tell us where we Christians have come from in the journey of faith. They tell us about a deep and unfolding relationship with a loving, if sometimes mystifying, God in a hundred different ways.

The Christian Scriptures, the New Testament, were shaped in a similar way but cover a much shorter time frame.

One way to understand this process of shaping Scripture is to imagine being part of a working group that is asked to develop a short film to capture the history of your school: Which photos and stories do you choose? Which ones do you omit? Who do you interview? Why? How do you put it all together? There will be unanimous agreement on some matters, and disagreement on others. *Good decisions will be made by reflecting on what most truly explains and reflects the spirit and story of your school.* You will know if you have done your job well by the reception your film receives.

The early Christian communities discerned similarly when they were gathering writings to shape what we now call the New Testament. Some writings, like many of the so-called Gnostic gospels, were excluded because they were less authentic. Others were accepted because, even though they may have been later writings, they were true to the community's understanding of Jesus and their experience of the Holy Spirit in the community. In other words, the early Church sought the guidance of the Holy Spirit in recognizing the work of the Holy Spirit. They wanted to gather inspired writings.

For these reasons, the Bible is considered as God's Word in human words. It is not meant to be an objective history of factual truths, even though it does record some significant historical details. Rather, the Bible is much more a remembrance of a romance with God: the wedding album, the love letters, the struggles and triumphs, the miracles and hopes. Some say the Bible is best understood as salvation history rather than social history. In other words, the stories are sometimes told to make a point, to express a divine truth that has been treasured and passed on through generations of the faith community.

The truths of the Bible are subtle rather than blunt. They are truths of grace. They emerge within the context of the entire Bible rather than in the narrow, possibly misleading frame of a single verse. Thus, the Vatican II document on revelation, *Dei Verbum*, states clearly,

The books of Scripture must be acknowledged as teaching solidly, faithfully and without error that truth which God wanted put into sacred writings for the sake of salvation....

However, since God speaks in Sacred Scripture through men in human fashion, the interpreter of Sacred Scripture, in order to see clearly what God wanted to communicate to us, should carefully investigate what meaning the sacred writers really intended, and what God wanted to manifest by means of their words.

To search out the intention of the sacred writers, attention should be given, among other things, to "literary forms." For truth is set forth and expressed differently in texts which are variously historical, prophetic, poetic, or of other forms of discourse....

The living tradition of the whole Church must be taken into account along with the harmony which exists between elements of the faith. (§§11–12)

This is a most important statement because it warns us against reading the Bible too literally or arguing from a single specific verse. Indeed, the Bible might at times be misleading if read at face value. For example, there are passages in the Bible about patriarchy, polygamy, the vengefulness of God, religious wars, laws of purity and exclusion, and so on, that seem repulsive today. We need to find, as Vatican II notes, "that truth which God wanted put into sacred writing for the sake of salvation."

The Bible is important, then, because it is the most precious possession of our faith community. It should be the first thing we take with us if we were being forced out of home, whether by fire or exile. Consider this inspiring story from Cardinal Nguyên Van Thuân, who was imprisoned by the communist government in Vietnam from 1975 to 1978:

In prison the Catholic prisoners divided the New Testament, which they had hidden and taken with them, into little sheets; they distributed them and learned them by heart. Since the ground was earth or sand, when the guards' steps were heard, the Word of God was hidden under earth. In the afternoon, at sundown, each one took turns reciting the part he knew; it was impressive and moving to hear the Word of God in the silence and darkness, the presence of Jesus, the 'living Gospel,' recited with all the soul's strength.[1]

This deep affection for the Bible is less common in an affluent Catholic Church. In my experience, young children love the selected Bible stories that they read in their religious education classes or act out in their Christmas liturgies. This is partly because the stories are written with words that children can easily understand alongside illustrations that engage the children's imagination.

Unfortunately, when children become adolescents, the reverse is often the case. The Bible becomes so uncool that it rarely evokes any response—except if it is presented through the selective interpretations of *Godspell* or *Joseph and the Amazing Technicolor Dreamcoat* or *Jesus Christ Superstar*. Young people, however, are not to blame for their lack of interest in the Bible. We adults may not treasure it enough ourselves and the readings in our liturgies often use overelaborate translations of unexplained texts that seem irrelevant. Too often, they are read without understanding, passion, and love. We need to do better.

There are exceptions, of course. I know good lectors who proclaim rather than mumble the word of God. They know the text by heart, literally, and every word they say is listened to. When pastors, readers, and teachers love the Bible, regarding it as a family treasure and knowing how to use it, then perhaps students may also take notice. I find that the story about the young man and his dog and angel always gets their attention.

---

1. Archbishop Nguyên Van Thuân, "Mission Moment," August 5, 2002, available online at http://missionmoment.blogspot .com/p/mission-moments-inspiring-quotes.html (accessed January 21, 2019).

3

IS FAITH REASONABLE?

Recently, a popular stand-up comedian called Sammy said, for the fifth or sixth time, that it was stupid to believe in some old man up in the sky, and that faith was, as he put it, "not intellectual but just emotional." What a wrongheaded and ill-informed view, not only of faith, but also of emotion. Why is intellectuality (his word) more important than emotion? And who says God is some old man up in the sky?

However, if that is the way Sammy has experienced people of faith, maybe people of faith are partly to blame for his ignorance. We should be teaching that faith is reasonable rather than anti-intellectual, and that it is personal and relational rather than just emotional. Furthermore, we should make it clear that God cannot be an old man up in the sky, because God is not limited by space and time, nor by gender or gravity. True, there is a sense in which God beholds us all, which can mean watching over us, but God is also as close to me as I am to myself. God cannot be reduced to an idol, a thing in a place, or to a gender. In speaking about faith in God, we need to focus on God being intimately present in our lives, inviting us into a friendship.

So, let us do some theology of faith. What is faith? Following the key steps for doing theology outlined in chapter 1, we start with the Bible. According to Scripture, faith is primarily personal and relational. Faith is about *whom* we believe in. We find many stories in Scripture about how people came to faith, beginning with Abraham and ending with St. Paul. In every case, their coming to faith rests on a personal encounter with the Lord God, or Jesus, or the Holy Spirit, or God's angels. Thus, in the middle chapters of the Book of Genesis, we learn how the Lord God appeared to Abraham, spoke to Abraham, instructed Abraham, made promises to Abraham, tested Abraham, and blessed Abraham. Abraham might have bowed to the ground before the Lord God and declared himself to be the Lord God's servant, but nevertheless, the Lord God became a regular visitor to Abraham's house and the two became best friends for life. They had a covenant between them.

Abraham's faith was not about *what* he believed, but *the one* he believed in. The Lord God had a name, *El Shaddai*, the God above all gods, the transcendent God, and yet this was the God who came to visit Abraham—a God, both transcendent and immanent, inviting Abraham into a friendship. His faith was not in a tin-pot idol, but rather "the LORD, the God of heaven" (Gen 24:7).

In the Gospels, we learn that Jesus finds faith in the outsiders who plead with him for help: the centurion, the paralytic, the woman with hemorrhages, the two blind men, and so on. He says to them, "Your faith has saved you." The disciples, however, are of "little faith," and those who keep testing him with questions are a "faithless and perverse generation." Faith clearly means believing *in* Jesus rather than believing *that* some statement is true. Thus, after Jesus's resurrection, the disciples come to a deep faith through a series of encounters with Jesus as the risen Lord.

When we consider Church tradition and teaching, our second step in doing theology, we find a greater focus on the "content of faith," or *what* it is that Christians believe. Not surprisingly, the *Catechism*, which is about teaching the contents of the faith, begins with a focus on Christian doctrine rather than on Jesus: "Catechesis is an education in the faith of children, young people and adults which includes especially the teaching of Christian doctrine" (§5).

If we look more carefully, though, we find that the *Catechism* insists on the priority of a personal relationship in faith: "Faith is first of all a personal adherence of man to God" and after that "a free assent to the whole truth that God has revealed" (§150). Faith *in* a person will always include words about their example and their teachings. The Church, guided by the Spirit of Jesus, sometimes has the task of clarifying these teachings in creeds and other declarations (or "propositions"). For these reasons, theologians say that faith is both "personal" and "propositional," both a belief *in* Jesus and a belief *that* the teachings of his Church are true.

If we are engaged in faith formation, we need the right balance. If we are unsure about our personal faith, it is easier in some ways to teach the contents of the faith—the propositions and practices.

But how can we teach a personal relationship? There are two important steps here. The first step in teaching a personal relationship in faith is to develop our own relationship with Jesus into a trusting friendship. How do we do this? How do we realize that Jesus is inviting each of us individually into a personal relationship? Often, we encounter the Lord in our own quiet moments of prayer, in reading the gospel, in the sacraments of the Church, among the community of the faithful, and particularly in the service of those who are poor, sick, imprisoned, and excluded. When times are difficult, we ask the Lord for help. When times are gloriously happy, we give praise to the Lord. And from day to day, we develop a closeness to Jesus: perhaps with a small icon on our desk, a crucifix on our wall, a small Sign of the Cross before a meal, some favorite prayers, and by mixing with other friends in the Lord at the Eucharist on Sunday. In doing this, we give our lives to Jesus. As we grow on the journey of faith, and as we grow older and wiser, we often become more reverent and devout as we grow closer to Jesus.

The second step in teaching a personal relationship with Jesus is to understand theologically that we cannot *make* children and young people have a relationship with Jesus. Faith cannot be constructed because faith is a gift from God. God always takes the initiative by coming to visit us, just as the Lord God visited Abraham near the great oak tree at Mamre, or just as Jesus met St. Paul on the road to Damascus. The Scriptures tell us that God offers this gift of self to every single person.

Every question we ask discloses our interest in the unknown; our desire to know more. Just as a child only asks for a Christmas present that she already knows about, so also, we seem to have an inbuilt sense of the infinite and constantly seek it. Theologians call this a gift of God that comes with being human. There is a long history of arguments about nature and grace, but the main point is that the role of the teacher is to help children see the invitation of God in love and beauty and life, and to help them find Jesus in their growing and learning. This is not hard because children are the ones who are "infinite openness to the infinite." The hard part is finding a way for the authentic faith of the Christian community to shine into the lives of children, young people, and their families. Our own example can increase this light.

In 2013, in one of the happiest collaborations of quite different theological minds, Pope Francis completed an encyclical letter on faith—*Lumen Fidei*—that had been largely written by Pope Benedict XVI before his retirement. The two popes together remind us that faith is born of a personal encounter, and that faith is always a journey alongside the one we believe in. Their encyclical letter begins:

> Faith is born of an encounter with the living God who calls us and reveals his love, a love which precedes us and upon which we can lean for security and for building our lives....Faith, received from God as a supernatural gift, becomes a light for our way, guiding our journey through time. On the one hand, it is a light coming from the past, the light of the foundational memory of the life of Jesus which revealed his perfectly trustworthy love, a love capable of triumphing over death. Yet since Christ has risen and draws

us beyond death, faith is also a light coming from the future and opening before us vast horizons which guide us beyond our isolated selves towards the breadth of communion. (§4)

So, is faith a delusion, a hallucination? My answer is a definite no. A delusion is an unreasonable take on reality, but faith is not unreasonable. While making a decision to believe in God may go *beyond* the evidence we currently have, it does not go *against* the evidence we have.

In our day-to-day lives, we are constantly making reasonable acts of faith: we catch a train or a bus, believing that it will take us to where it says it is going. We buy food in tins and jars, believing that the contents will match the label. This faith is reasonable rather than unreasonable. But we also buy health care products, believing they will make us young and vibrant, and this doesn't always work! Many great delusions of our lives come in consumer advertising, where what we are promised turns out to be nothing like what we end up buying.

Faith can be tested by its fruits. We make a reasonable act of faith when we commit to another person in marriage. We come to know the person and their family and the way they love and live. We receive their love and understanding. All things point to a happy future, but making our commitment remains an act of faith because the future is still to come.

For Christians, faith is not in a purely theoretical God, but in a God who comes among us—an earthling like us. Commitment to Jesus is like commitment to a partner in marriage: on the strength of Jesus's love, in the real context of doubt and persecution, we choose to follow.

Our faith in God can be shaken. The more we make God in our own image, the more we will be disappointed when God turns out to be different from what we had expected. Furthermore, sometimes bad things happen to good people. Sometimes our prayers are not answered. Sometimes the cruel prosper and the poor are massacred. How can faith in a good God be reasonable in those moments? The answers to some of these questions are attempted in the chapters that follow, but, in the end, God is always greater than we can imagine, and we live by faith.

Faith is not unreasonable, but it goes beyond reason because it is ultimately a commitment to a person. Faith thus requires something of us: hearing and doing. Faith does involve a leap into the unknown, like any commitment to a relationship, but it is an informed leap. We are asked by Jesus to make this leap, to have faith *in* him.

4

CAN EXPRESSIONS OF FAITH CHANGE?

In the fourth century, St. Augustine wrote that *Ecclesia semper reformanda est*—"The Church is always reforming." In announcing the new *Catechism of the Catholic Church* in 1992, Pope John Paul II noted that "the faith is always the same yet the source of ever new light."[1] In other words, while the faith is "always the same" (*semper eadem*), it shines new light in every new age. Sometimes newfangled ideas must be corrected, and sometimes the faith needs to be better explained. The Church's teaching developed through the early years of Christianity, most notably at the Council of Nicaea (325) and the Council of Chalcedon (451).

As noted in chapter 1, in theology, we often need to hold contradictions together. Here is a case in point. On the one hand, it is true to say that our faith is always the same because it is always faith in the same Jesus Christ. On the other hand, it is also true to say that expressions of the faith may change as times and circumstances change. Vatican II, for example, begins with the intention of finding out "how we ought to renew ourselves."[2] If the Church is the pilgrim people of God, then we are on a journey, and there is still much to learn.

It is one thing to say that expressions of faith may change, but another thing to say that Church teaching can change. Some theologians and Church authorities argue for what John Henry Newman called the "Development of Doctrine," which proposes that new teachings clarify and enhance earlier teachings, rather than undermining them. Other theologians argue for what is sometimes called a "Hierarchy of Truths," which means that there are core teachings that will never change, but that there are also less-central teachings, such as those that relate to regulation of practices, which may well change. Pope Francis thus observes,

---

1. John Paul II, *Fidei Depositum* (1992).
2. From the "Message to Humanity" issued at the beginning of the Second Vatican Council (1962).

All revealed truths derive from the same divine source and are to be believed with the same faith, yet some of them are more important for giving direct expression to the heart of the Gospel. In this basic core, what shines forth is the beauty of the saving love of God made manifest in Jesus Christ who died and rose from the dead. In this sense, the Second Vatican Council explained, "in Catholic doctrine there exists an order or a 'hierarchy' of truths, since they vary in their relation to the foundation of the Christian faith." (*Evangelii Gaudium* 36)[3]

History tells us that while the faith may remain the same, Church teaching does indeed change. Consider, for example, whether bishops should be married or not. The First Letter of Timothy tells us that "a bishop must be above reproach, married only once, temperate, sensible, respectable, hospitable, an apt teacher, not a drunkard, not violent but gentle, not quarrelsome, and not a lover of money (1 Tim 3:2–3). St. John Chrysostom (ca. 349–407), Archbishop of Constantinople, did not take this to mean that a bishop should be married, but rather that a bishop should only be married once.[4] In the same century, however, Pope Siricius (384–99) and the Synod or Council in Carthage (ca. 390) taught that bishops and priests, though married, should observe perfect chastity. St. Ambrose (ca. 340–97), the bishop of Milan, agreed, arguing that the letter to Timothy was not talking about bishops begetting children, but about bishops who had children. By the time of the papacy of St. Leo the Great (440–61), the law of celibacy was being promulgated in the Western or Latin Catholic Church, though not recognized in the Eastern Greek Catholic Church. Here we see considerable changes in teaching by bishops and about bishops!

There are also several notorious instances where Church teaching has changed in relation to the natural sciences. Galileo was condemned because, among other things, his view that the earth rotated around the sun appeared to contradict the Bible's teaching that the sun moved around the heavens. It is only fair to note that Galileo's theory also went against common sense because the sun did indeed appear to move around the heavens. Very few people accepted Galileo's views during his lifetime. Eventually, in 1992, John Paul II conceded that Galileo had been "imprudently opposed."

---

3. Referring to Vatican II, *Unitatis Redintegratio*, §11.
4. St. John Chrysostom, Homily on 1 Timothy 3:1–4.

A less well-known case concerns Pope Zacharius in 748. Some scholars had been arguing that the earth was round rather than flat and that there might be people living in the Antipodes (or Down Under). Pope Zacharius then put a ban on the idea of the Antipodes and their human occupation, describing this as "a perverse and iniquitous doctrine." The idea of the Antipodes was rejected on two grounds: first, because it opposed common sense—the earth did seem flat, and it was hard to imagine how people could live upside down or rain could fall upward; and, second, because it opposed the biblical teaching that all would see the Lord when he came down from heaven again (see Rev 1:7). In our own time, understanding how to read the Bible (see chapter 2) and understanding the value of the truth of science have allowed the Church to reread Scripture and change its own teaching about matter and the cosmos.

The Latin word for "teacher" is *magister*. The teaching office of the Church, as exercised by the pope and the bishops, is thus called the "magisterium." While some may see the magisterium as a conservative body, its very existence implies that the Church's teaching is not fixed, and that new times may require "ever new light."

If it is right to resist "change for change's sake," it may also be wrong to resist change that has been prompted by the Holy Spirit and authorized through the teaching office of the Church. This does not mean that the Church's teaching lacks firm foundations. There are core elements of faith that will never be changed, such as the incarnation and resurrection of Jesus, though they may be authentically expressed in new ways.

Though the Church moves slowly, and too slowly for some, authentic teaching in matters of faith is a complicated process that does take time. It sometimes requires humility and humor—as well as faith in Jesus—to accept resistance to change. Even when we might think the teaching of the Church is wrong, there are ways to abide faithfully in the Church. Let me conclude with two examples of abiding faith in the Church.

First, there is the story of Dorothy Day (1897–1980), the cofounder of the Catholic Worker Movement, an advocate for nonviolence, an opponent of the exploitation of workers and the poor, and a creator of communities for the homeless. On the one hand, she accepted the teaching of the Church on marriage and so had to separate herself from the love of her life and the father of her daughter because he refused to enter into marriage. On the other hand, she spoke out against bishops and archbishops who supported militarism. She sometimes felt the institutional Church let her down. And yet, with great forbearance, she kept her focus on her faith in Jesus. She would write, "I love the Church with all my heart and soul....I have never wanted to challenge the Church, only be part of it, obey it, and in return, receive its mercy and love, the mercy and love of Jesus."[5]

Second, there is the story of Roland Walls (1918–2011), an Anglican priest who became a Catholic priest. He had founded an ecumenical Christian community in Scotland, gathering people from many denominations, but he could not persuade any Roman Catholics to join him. He knew his community was incomplete, so at the age of sixty-four, he decided to become a Roman Catholic himself, and asked to be ordained as a Catholic priest. Because Roland had been a Professor of New Testament at Cambridge University, Cardinal Gray of Edinburgh wisely decided that he did not need any further seminary training. Instead, he sent Roland away for three months to reflect on the documents of Vatican II. When Roland returned, the Cardinal asked, "So, what did you make of the documents?" Roland replied, "I think they're full of unexploded bombs which have never been discovered," he replied, "and which will go off at some point."[6] Roland was a radical. He understood that Church teaching was not so much about locking us into the past as about giving us direction into the future.

It helps if we understand that the Church is much more than Church teaching, much more than the pope and the bishops, the so-called hierarchical or institutional Church. The Church is primarily the community of the disciples of Jesus, drawn together by the Holy Spirit since the first Pentecost, continuing the work of Jesus. Catholic teaching thus speaks of there being two dimensions to the Church. One dimension is named after St. Peter and is called the Petrine dimension of the Church. The Petrine dimension follows from the ministry of Peter as pastor and teacher, leader and priest, and it continues in the ministry of the pope and bishops and priests today. The second dimension is named after Mary, the Mother of Jesus, and is called the Marian dimension of the Church. The Marian dimension reflects the life of Mary and the community gathered with Mary at Pentecost: this dimension of Church is open to the Holy Spirit—prayerful, serving others, bound by love to Jesus, inclusive, a community of equals, lay, faithful, and holy.

One of the "unexploded bombs" in the *Catechism of the Catholic Church*, is that

---

5. Robert Coles, *Dorothy Day: A Radical Devotion* (New York: Da Capo Press, 1989), 82–84.
6. See John Miller, *A Simple Life: Roland Walls and the Community of the Transfiguration* (Edinburgh: St. Andrew Press, 2014), 177.

"the 'Marian' dimension of the Church precedes the 'Petrine'" (§773). In other words, the Marian dimension could be described as the underlying faith that always remains the same, the heart of the Church, attuned to Jesus, guided by the Holy Spirit. The strength of this mystical union makes change in teaching possible, as guided by the pope and the bishops.

Part Two

QUESTIONS ABOUT GOD

5

WHY IS GOD CALLED "GOD"?

The word *honey* has no real meaning until you have tasted honey. The same can be said of the word *God*. But how do we taste God? What can we say?

An ant cannot say much about a human being. Nor can human beings say much about God. All talk about God is complicated. By any account, God is a being much more complex than we are, and much greater than we can imagine. However, human beings can think and talk, so we must try to say something. We point at things and give them names. Honey...God.

Personal names are important. They make connections. Children are much more direct about asking each other their names, and they are very good at remembering names. For them, there seems to be a direct link between knowing a name and knowing who someone is. They become best friends. It is not surprising, therefore, that children want to know about how God got a name, especially if God is a person rather than a thing.

Our English word *God*, however, is not the *name of* the Divine Creator, but *our word for* the Divine Creator. We know that this word, *God*, comes from very early Germanic languages and was used to translate the Latin word *Deus* and the Greek word *Theos*, but we have no certain knowledge of what *God* means. Perhaps it refers to something noble, valued, worshipped. All these words—*Theos, Deus, God*—refer to a being much greater than we are. The French have a more open-ended and melodic word for "God"—*Dieu*. But *God* and *Dieu* are not names so much as pointing words.

I live almost next door to a primary school. Often, when I am out walking with our dog, Maddie, I run into children with their parents or grandparents on their way to or from school. Maddie is a very friendly dog, and she wags her tail whenever she sees children. "Can I pet your dog?" the children ask politely. And then, as they pet and cuddle Maddie, they then always ask, "What's his name, what kind of dog is he, how old is he?" Slightly miffed at their gendered language, I say, "She's a girl dog, and her name is Maddie. She is a spoodle, and she is nearly twelve years old." They say, "Hello, Maddie." Sometimes I then say, "She loves a hello, but she can't see you: she is blind." The children go, "Ooooh." They've made a connection. They never forget Maddie.

There is a lot of dog-walking where I live. We regularly cross paths with the same people walking the same dogs. We get to know the dogs by name, but not the people. After several months of these meetings, as trust grows, we begin to share our own names. Friendships grow, sharing grows, and community grows. This is oddly different from what happens when I go to a conference, where we all have name tags, introduce ourselves, and say something about our work. As someone once joked, these days it is a sign of intimacy to know a person's second name.

If we take our first theological step and reflect on what Scripture tells us about God's name, we will find a wonderful treasury of stories, poems, and wisdom. In the opening chapters of the Book of Genesis, we find that God has two different names. In most English translations of Genesis, we find the words "The Lord" or "God" or "The Lord God," but the original Hebrew texts are a little more revealing. In the first chapter of Genesis, with the seven days of Creation, God is called *Elohim*, but in most of the second chapter, which contains the story of Adam and Eve, God is called *YHWH-Elohim*.

The chosen people regarded the name of their God as being so holy that it was too sacred to be pronounced or written. So, instead of giving God's full name, the Scriptures only give the consonants, as in YHWH, without the vowels. To use a trivial example, if I told the children our dog is called MDD, they would never work out her real name is Maddie.

Elsewhere in the Bible, there are other names for God: *Adonai*, which means "Lord," and *El Shaddai*, which means something like "God above all Gods," often poorly translated into English as God Almighty. In other words, our English word *God* is a very limited translation of the name of the Divine Creator.

In the time of Abraham, maybe four thousand years ago, there were many tribes, each with their own god. That local god was often an idol made of stone or wood that the people revered and carried around with them. Some groups had both a good god and an evil god. These were very limited gods, and some of them were called "El." The God that Abraham met, however, was quite different, saying, "I am *El Shaddai*" ("the God above all other gods," see Gen 17:1). In other words, this God was not an idol. This name was above all other names, and this God was above all the other gods.

Many generations later, when the children of Abraham were in slavery in Egypt, Moses encountered a divine presence in a burning bush that did not burn itself out. Moses then asked,

> "If I come to the Israelites and say to them, 'The God of your ancestors has sent me to you,' and they ask me, 'What is his name?' what shall I say to them?" God said to Moses, "I AM WHO I AM." He said further, "Thus you shall say to the Israelites, 'I AM has sent me to you.'" God also said to Moses, "Thus you shall say to the Israelites, 'The LORD [YHWH], the God of your ancestors, the God of Abraham, the God of Isaac, and the God of Jacob, has sent me to you':
>
> This is my name forever,
> and this my title for all generations."

(Exod 3:13–15)

From then on in the Hebrew Scriptures, the name of God is revered as holy mystery. The Lord God is described through many images—shepherd, potter, lover, vine owner, father, mother, creator, king, gentle wind, mighty fortress—and at the same time is reverenced as being beyond human comprehension.

The English word *God* is a generic word like the word *car*, rather than a specific name like *El Shaddai* or Rolls Royce. However, God is the name we reach for when we are amazed or in need. How often do we cry out "Oh my God" and "God help us"? So, in a way, God has become our personal name for the Divine Being. I don't think God would mind what name we use, as long as we are growing in our personal relationship, but perhaps we could show God more reverence: God is not just a name; God is a person ecstatically in love with me.

Christians believe Jesus shows us the face and heart of the God of Abraham and the God of Moses. Jesus does this with such perfect love that he is believed to be the unique incarnation of God. As Jesus said to Philip, "Whoever has seen me has seen the Father" (John 14:9). Jesus teaches us to call God "Our Father." This is not to say that God is some old man in the clouds, or that God has male gender, but that we owe our being to God, and that God cares about us, and that God is ecstatically in love with each one of us, as any parent is with their child. The Prophet Isaiah thus reports God's maternal care for us:

Listen to me, O house of Jacob,
all the remnant of the house of Israel,
who have been borne by me from your birth,
carried from the womb;
even to your old age I am he,
even when you turn gray I will carry you.
I have made, and I will bear;
I will carry and will save.

(Isa 46:3–4)

The Bible is currently arranged in the books of Moses, the books of the Law, the books of the Prophets, and so on. Scripture scholarship has also made it possible for us to read the Bible in historical order. When you read the Bible this way, it is interesting to note how the central image of God changes from a sometimes harsh patriarchal God who promises victory in battle to a compassionate God who shepherds his people even in exile, and then to an incarnate God who gives his life for us.

While God doesn't have or need a name, it is wonderful for each of us, in our own spiritual journey, to find our own name for God, to get to know God better. If we have truly encountered God, we will certainly use God's name with a deeper reverence. Blaise Pascal (1623–62) had such an encounter. He was a famous French scientist responsible for mechanical calculators and binomial coefficients, as well as Pascal's Principle, but God was more important to him than all his learning. After his death, a small scrap of paper was found in the lining of his coat. It describes his mystical encounter with God (*Dieu*). Translated into English, it reads in part,

The year of grace 1654,
Monday, 23 November....
From about half past ten at night until about half past midnight,

FIRE
GOD of Abraham, GOD of Isaac, GOD of Jacob
not of the philosophers and of the learned.
Certitude. Certitude. Feeling. Joy. Peace.
GOD of Jesus Christ.
My God and your God.
Your GOD will be my God....

Righteous Father, the world has not known you, but I have known you.
Joy, joy, joy, tears of joy....
This is eternal life, that they know you, the one true God,
and the one that you sent, Jesus Christ.
Jesus Christ.
Jesus Christ....
May I not forget your words. Amen.

This is the taste of God, like the taste of honey, that gives real meaning to the word *God*. When we meet the God above all gods—it might be in our own mystical moment or in a time of great need—we will know God and the mystery of God, just like Pascal. While we are on the way to that encounter, we can use names like Dear God, Almighty God, Loving Creator, Beloved Father—the God above all gods will hear them all. Better than that, even though we might be unsure about God's name, in faith we can be sure God knows each one of us by name. God knows who we are. God does not need to ask our name.

6

IF GOD MADE THE WORLD, WHO MADE GOD?

This is a relatively easy question to answer if you can stretch your brain around the issues involved.

The question usually arises when a teacher tries to prove that God must exist because everything must have a cause, and so ultimately there must be a first cause, and this first cause is what we call God.

The smart student will quickly point out the lack of consistency here: "But you just said that everything must have a cause, so what caused God?"

After congratulating the student on her intelligence, a teacher might first explain that everything we can observe in our world seems to have been caused by something preceding it. But this cannot go on forever, so there must be a different kind of being that is an uncaused cause, and this we call God.

For example, many of the things with which we are familiar have been made by someone else: the school is built by builders, our food comes from farmers, our clothes are made from wool and cotton and synthetic fibers, which come from sheep and cotton farms and chemical engineers. Cars and computers come from factories. Toys come from shops, and so on. And the things in nature seem to come from something else: bushes and trees grow from seeds, the seeds come from fruit and flowers. Birds come from eggs and the eggs come from dinosaurs. Rivers come from melted snow and rain, beaches are made by waves breaking on rocks, light and heat come from the sun, the moon shapes the tides, and the billions of stars in the hundred billion galaxies in the sky have come into being out of the consolidation of the big bang. It seems that everything that "is" has been caused by, or depends on, some being that preceded it. The cause is not just a material or physical cause—like wool or factory—

but also often includes a purpose: we make clothes because we want to keep warm; we make food because we need to eat, and so on.

First, a teacher could ask if anyone can think of a being that is not caused by something else, a being that is its own explanation. A clever student might suggest that love or truth or beauty do not seem to be caused. A very clever student might suggest that pure "being" does not have to be caused, because "being," by definition, already "is."

Second, a teacher might point out that there are levels of being: a flower is a more complex being than a rock; an insect is a more complex being than a flower; a fish is a more complex being than an insect; a bird is a more complex being than a fish; a kangaroo is a more complex being than a bird; and a human being seems to be the most complex of animals. But just as a rock cannot imagine an insect, an insect cannot imagine a fish, and fish cannot imagine a bird, a human being struggles to imagine that there might be some higher form of being. But why couldn't there be higher forms of being? Anyone for angels?

The highest form of being would be a being that is its own explanation, whose "being" is "to be." It needs no cause because it just "is." This is not a proof of the existence of God, but it is a reasonable way of thinking about the possibility of a being that does not need to be made and does not need to have a cause.

This metaphysical way of thinking of God as "pure being" fits conveniently with God's revelation to Moses—"I AM WHO I AM"—as discussed in the previous chapter. The metaphysical account of God as pure being, however, is more an abstract God of the philosophers rather than the personal God of Abraham and Moses.

The metaphysical way of thinking, because it was so abstract, went out of fashion with the success of modern science, which dealt with concrete objects rather than philosophical ideas. After all, who has ever seen pure being? In more recent years, however, postmodern philosophers have argued that our scientific words paper over deeper, and perhaps unknowable, realms. Some French postmodern philosophers are thus said to have taken a "theological turn." Postmodern philosophy and the metaphysics of the scholastic philosophers of the Middle Ages thus have much in common: they see the universe as less knowable or more mysterious than did the so-called modern scientists and philosophers of the Enlightenment.[1]

I would argue that it is reasonable to imagine the possibility of a being that is its own explanation. If such a being existed, then it would not need a cause. God could

---

1. For those interested in this complex topic, the writings of John D. Caputo are particularly illuminating. See, e.g., his *The Prayers and Tears of Jacques Derrida* (Bloomington: Indiana University Press, 1997).

be such a being. This is a god of the philosophers, perhaps, rather than the God of Abraham, but philosophy gives us another angle on the being of God.

At this stage, some student might reasonably use the "H" word—*hallucination*—or its equivalent, to suggest that we are just dreaming if we think something can be its own explanation. Here you can clap your hands with joy and play the science card, because according to the big bang theory, as Stephen Hawking put it, the universe needs no explanation: it "would have neither beginning nor end: it would simply be."[2]

Do not exult too much, however, because the big bang theory then raises another question: If the universe can be its own explanation, what need do we have for a creator? We will say more about this in chapter 11.

---

2. Stephen Hawking, *A Brief History of Time* (London: Bantam, 1988), 149. For more on how the universe needs no external cause, see the following chapter.

7

DID GOD REALLY MAKE THE WORLD IN SEVEN DAYS?

The Big Bang Theory is one of the most watched television shows of all time. The episodes begin with a theme song that tells the story of evolution and ends with the chorus, "It all started with the big bang."

Children and young people are genuinely interested in how the world came into being. They like the idea that the world is made just for them by a loving God. The older they get, however, the more skeptical they become about the world being made in seven days. They believe more in evolution than they do in Eve and Adam. Many students see a very serious mismatch between what they get taught in science classes and what they get taught in religion classes. Some are swayed by the writings of the new atheists, like Richard Dawkins, who see the Bible as "just plain weird."

So, which account of the origins of the universe do we believe—the big bang theory or the Book of Genesis? My answer is that we can believe both.

We believe the big bang theory to be the most plausible scientific account of *how* our universe came to be, even though scientists accept that the theory may be modified or revised in future years. It is also worth letting students know that the big bang theory was first proposed around 1930 by a Belgian Catholic priest and cosmologist, Georges Lemaître, who argued that the universe expanded from an initial point that he called the "Primeval Atom." His critics mocked him by calling his idea the big bang theory—even Einstein thought it was an implausible theory—and the name stuck after Lemaître's theory became more widely accepted.

The big bang theory and modified versions of Darwin's theory of evolution give a coherent though not completely proven account of *how* the universe came into being and *how* life evolved on our planet, but these scientific accounts do not explain *why* there is a universe, or *why* human life came to be. As far as science is concerned, the universe stems from a self-explanatory if random event called the big bang.

The Genesis accounts of Creation take a different approach to the *how* and *why* of Creation. It is a mistake to read the Genesis accounts of Creation as if they were contemporary scientific theories. This is clear when we realize that Genesis gives us two quite different stories of how the universe was created.

The Book of Genesis begins with the story of Creation over seven days (Gen 1:1— 2:3), where God seems to be *outside* creation. This story, nonetheless, has some basis in experience and observation because it matches the experience of someone waking up at first light and gradually seeing more detail in the world. Chapter 2 offers quite a different story about Creation over one day, where God moves *in* the created world and the features of creation come into being in a different order from the first account. The focus of this story is on the origin and purpose of human beings, as characterized by Adam and Eve (Gen 2:4–24). The point of these stories is *that there is a creator* who created with intention and delight and tasked Adam (a word that could mean "the ruddy skinned one" or "a man" or even "humankind") with caring for all creation.

This notion of a personal creator is the "truth which God wanted put into sacred writings for the sake of salvation," to quote from Vatican II (see also chapter 2 on the Bible). Later Church teaching makes the same point. Consider Pope Francis's address to a gathering at the Pontifical Academy of Sciences in 2014:

> When we read the account of Creation in Genesis, we risk imagining that God was a magician, complete with an all powerful magic wand. But that was not so. He created beings and he let them develop according to the internal laws with which He endowed each one, that they might develop, and reach their fullness. He gave autonomy to the beings of the universe at the same time in which He assured them of his continual presence, giving life to every reality. And thus Creation has been progressing for centuries and centuries, millennia and millennia, until becoming as we know it today, precisely because God is not a demiurge or a magician, but the Creator who gives life to all beings.

A particularly important part of the second Genesis account of Creation is that God walks in the Garden with Adam and Eve and speaks with them by name. In other words, this Creator God has a special relationship with us, is on first-name terms with us. Pope Francis makes this point in his encyclical letter *Laudato Si'*:

> Human beings, even if we postulate a process of evolution, also possess a uniqueness which cannot be fully explained by the evolution of other open systems. Each of us has his or her own personal identity and is capable of entering into dialogue with others and with God....The biblical accounts of creation invite us to see each human being as a subject who can never be reduced to the status of an object. (§81)

In faith we believe that the universe not only has a physical cause—the *how*—but also purpose or intent, namely, God's desire to create a community of love. Physics suggests that there is possibly an almost infinite number of parallel universes, and that ours might be the only universe that has the elegant design of life as we know it. But *why*? The running joke of *The Big Bang Theory* television series—and perhaps unfair to physicists—is that the scientists understand the physics but struggle to comprehend the love.

A CONCLUDING SCIENTIFIC POSTSCRIPT

Students and teachers who really want to stretch their brains, especially those who know some physics, might find it helpful to understand the big bang theory, and how—contrary to Isaac Newton—there is no abiding structure of space and time into which the universe has been fitted. Space and time unfold with the unfolding of matter. Space and time did not exist prior to our universe. There was nothing physical prior to the universe.

How can this be so? We are all quite familiar with Einstein's famous equation: $E = mc^2$. This is the equation that explains nuclear energy and nuclear bombs, where E is energy, m is mass, and c is the speed of light. The speed of light is approximately 300,000 km/s (186,000 mi/s), so c^2 becomes a very large number (around 90,000,000,000). Therefore, a small amount of mass, multiplied by this large number, can produce an enormous amount of energy, for good or bad, for nuclear energy or, as we hope never to experience, for nuclear weapons.

Physicists do not know very much about the first moment of the big bang, from zero to 10^{-43} seconds, called the Planck era. However, this instant may rest on a similar equation to Einstein's equation. This equation is called Planck's equation—$E = h\nu$—which relates the energy in a photon of light (E) to the frequency of the light (ν), meaning the number of vibrations of a wave per a period of time, in this case seconds.

In this equation, $\hbar$ is a constant number, called Planck's constant. All you need to understand about this equation is that there is an essential relationship between energy and time: as time gets smaller and smaller, energy gets bigger and bigger. And if time gets almost infinitely small, so that it is virtually nonexistent, then energy gets almost infinitely large. And that is perhaps the first stage of the big bang: where there is nothing and virtually no time, and with some complex physics, there could be an eruption of almost infinite energy. This energy then condenses into the building blocks of matter and the subsequent unfolding of our universe over 14 billion years until it is as we know it today.

8

SO WHERE IS GOD?

Ask the students if any of them have a cat. Then ask them if their cat barks loudly. I wager they will protest, "Don't be silly, cats don't bark." The same could be said if a child asks, "So where is God?" We could answer, "Don't be silly, God doesn't have a body like we do, so God can't be in a place like we are." God is not in a specific place.

We can, however, talk about the presence of God. My best friend can be personally present to me even though she might be some distance away in space and time. In our faith, God is as near to me as I am to myself. Just as "blueness" is present in everything that is blue—blue sky, blue sea, blue cars, blue clothes—so, it also seems reasonable to argue that "being" is present in every kind of being. If God is the one who *is*, or "pure being," then we can imagine that wherever there is "isness"—or being—then God is present.

"But if God doesn't have a body, how can God be real?"

Reality is more than bodily reality. Wi-Fi is real, but it has no body. Love and truth are real, but they don't occupy a specific place. The fundamental constituents of matter—the things that make up electrons and protons and neutrons—are called quarks. But we can't see quarks. They have names like "charm" and "strange" because they don't have bodies. Whether we are thinking about quarks or thinking about God, we need to stretch our brains: some elements of reality are not material in the simple sense of being bodies with mass in space and time.[1]

"But how do we know God is not just something we humans have made up?"

Are Superman and Wonder Woman real? Not really! We know they are not real because we know they were made up by people who wrote comics and then made films with lots of computer-generated images for effect. Is Santa Claus real? Yes and no, maybe... Yes, because there was a St. Nicholas who did give needy families gifts

---

1. If we really wanted to bamboozle students, and bamboozle ourselves, we could point out that according to the tests of Bell's theorem and quantum entanglement, our stretched-out frameworks of time and space conceal the deeper reality that nature is essentially and instantaneously entangled, and that we are more connected than we are separate.

at Christmas. No, because all the shopping associated with Christmas has fake Santa Clauses with fake beards, and for the most part has covered over the memory of Jesus with snow and reindeers.

"Well wasn't God just invented the same way, only a long time ago?"

Good question, but what's different is that the people who invented the superheroes clearly didn't believe they really existed; but the people who talked about God clearly believed that God did exist: they had had an encounter with God, a taste of God.

Human beings do have strange experiences that take them out of body and out of space and time. This happens most obviously in dreams, but these experiences can happen when we are awake. These are sometimes described as mystical experiences—or extraordinary experiences—of the transcendent. *Transcendent* means something like "beyond our ordinary physical experience." *Transcendent* is the opposite of *immanent*, which means what we can touch and see, what is at hand.

Our Bible has many stories about people encountering the transcendent and believing in God: Abraham welcomes God as a kind of angelic visitor; Moses finds God in a burning bush that never burns out. God may be similarly experienced in our day-to-day lives. God's presence is always slightly filtered, slightly unreal.

The most memorable story of an encounter with God is that of Elijah, who was told to go to Mount Horeb to meet the Lord. We read,

> Now there was a great wind, so strong that it was splitting mountains and breaking rocks in pieces before the LORD, but the LORD was not in the wind; and after the wind an earthquake, but the LORD was not in the earthquake; and after the earthquake a fire, but the LORD was not in the fire; and after the fire a sound of sheer silence. When Elijah heard it, he wrapped his face in his mantle and went out and stood at the entrance of the cave. Then there came a voice to him that said, "What are you doing here, Elijah?" (1 Kgs 19:11–13)

There is an important lesson here. To sense the presence of God—and God is always present—we need to let God find us. We must go beyond our five usual senses (seeing, hearing, tasting, smelling, touching) and be open to a deeper sense. This "sixth sense" used to be called a "spiritual sense," though today we sometimes speak of it as intuition, extrasensory perception, or emotional intelligence. Elijah, with his spiritual sense, heard God in the silence.

Even though children and adolescents are in many ways complex creatures who are hungry for sensory experiences, they can take to silence and be amazed by, even overwhelmed by, the wonder and mystery of life. Our consumer culture does us all a disservice by selling us cheap substitutes in our quest for transcendence. Teachers have a duty to help young people develop their own spiritual sense, encouraging them to enjoy the mystical and to grow spiritually along their own God-given path. The mystical is the place where we can explore the meaning of our lives. We may possibly be encountered by God and get a deeper sense of the secret meaning of our being.

I remember as a teenager going for walks at night, trying to work out who I was and what I was meant to do. On one occasion, I stopped on a bridge and looked down into the waters below. It was a calm clear night. As I looked down into the mirror surface of the water, I could see below me all the bright stars of the sky above. In that moment of being surrounded by stars, both above me and below me, I had a profound experience of the sacred. From that moment, it has been easy for me to find the real presence of God in my life. God is as close to me as I am to myself, here and now.

One of the best ways to teach children and young people to find God is to help them develop their sixth sense, their spiritual sense. We can develop a child's musical sense by giving them piano or guitar lessons. The more music they learn, the more they can recognize different keys, different chords, and different tempos. Their ear becomes attuned. When they hear a musical chord, they can immediately hear whether it is a major chord, a minor chord, or a diminished seventh, and so on. They can do this because, with the help of an experienced teacher, they have developed their sense of hearing. We can similarly help a child develop his or her spiritual sense.

This could begin, for example, with Godly play, or reflection on the beauty and mysticism of nature, or doing meditation, learning prayers, and so on. Children are naturally full of wonder. Their wonder is a spiritual sense of the greatness and beauty of being.

Helping children explore their sense of God works best, of course, if the teacher has done some spiritual exercises too! Otherwise teaching spirituality is as useless as a music teacher who has never played an instrument.

We can help children and young people identify their own spiritual journeys. A good spiritual teacher has a sense of spiritual truth. A teacher was seen sitting in silence while watching a boy practice his diving at a school swimming pool. When asked why he was doing this, the teacher explained that the boy had said he felt closest to God when he was diving, and so the teacher was sharing the experience with him.

One of the aberrations of religion is that we domesticate God, tie God down to a specific place, like a church or a temple. We can't have God in our pocket. We need to let God surprise us. While it is perfectly good to have focal points for the gathering and celebrations of the faithful, and to have places of reverence and beauty that point to the mystery and holiness of God, we should be ready to meet God anywhere.

There is a beautiful story in the Gospel of John when Jesus meets the Samaritan woman and they argue about many things, including where God is to be encountered. We read,

> The woman said to him, "Sir, I see that you are a prophet. Our ancestors worshiped on this mountain, but you say that the place where people must worship is in Jerusalem." Jesus said to her, "Woman, believe me, the hour is coming when you will worship the Father neither on this mountain nor in Jerusalem....But the hour is coming, and is now here, when the true worshipers will worship the Father in spirit and truth, for the Father seeks such as these to worship him." (John 4:19–23)

So where is God to be found? "Neither on this mountain nor in Jerusalem." God is present everywhere, especially in each person's heart, in love and spirit and truth.

For Christians, God is found in and through Jesus, especially in the faith community where two or three are gathered in his name, and in the service of the poor. Tricky questions about Jesus and about the Church, however, may be topics for another book.

9

IF GOD IS ALMIGHTY, WHY IS THERE SO MUCH SUFFERING?

When we are experiencing great suffering, particularly the suffering of our loved ones, our first response should be to care rather than to philosophize, to feel rather than to think, and to comfort rather than to explain. This tricky question about why there is so much suffering is nonetheless often asked. In short, the answer is that we suffer because we are *limited* physical beings who have *unlimited* hope for perfect happiness; every time we experience a limitation—like running into a wall—we suffer.

But why does God allow this? The short answer is that God is almighty in love, and love entails suffering. That is why the cross is central to our faith.

In Christian faith, God is not a puppet master and we are not puppets. God gives us bodies with self-protecting nerves, but nerves entail pain. God gives us freedom to make our own choices, but freedom entails risk and hurt. God gives us the power of love, but love can break our hearts and destroy our spirit. God lets nature take its course, its own cycles and seasons, but this unfolding of life entails natural disasters.

We can try to buffer ourselves against pain. Recently, I went to a bubble-soccer birthday party for seven-year-old girls and boys in a local park. The girls and boys got strapped inside big inflated plastic doughnuts and ran around on a grass field that was surrounded by inflated rubber walls. They ran hard at each other, bounced about, did random somersaults, but were completely safe. Everyone was protected. All the same, one boy got sick from being left upside down too long. Another boy cried because his best friend ran into him too hard when he didn't expect it. His *feelings* were hurt! It seems impossible to protect ourselves from pain forever.

The children eventually got tired of being buffered. They climbed out of their plastic doughnuts, ran off to another part of the park, and climbed up into what they called the magic tree. Here, there was neither safety net nor climbing harness—much to the consternation of some parents. The children climbed higher and higher. We couldn't get them to come down until the birthday cake was being cut. If they had fallen from that tree, they might have hurt themselves. All we grown-ups could do was watch. The children came down safe and happy.

We love children so much that we do everything we can to keep them safe. The children, however, love being free to explore and take risks. Sometimes they get hurt. We pick them up and comfort them. Sometimes we interfere and end their games: "No, you can't ride your skateboard...down the middle of the road...without a helmet...being towed by your friend on a bicycle...carrying your dog...in peak hour traffic...at night...facing backward...." "Why not?" they reply, with deep sighs.

We can't keep everybody safe. We can't completely stop young people from taking risks. We can't always stop tyrants from causing wars. We can't stop greedy people from causing displacement, poverty, and disease. We can't always stop troubled souls lighting wild fires, dealing drugs, causing road rage, and setting off seemingly endless cycles of suffering.

This kind of suffering arises because of the choices people make. All the same, a child can rightly ask, "Isn't God still to blame? Why did God have to make us this way? And what about completely innocent suffering, such as children being born with terrible diseases? Why can't God do something about that? Why are there over fifty million displaced persons and refugees on our planet, with so many of them being innocent children? Why must good people have to bear terrible burdens? Why do some families experience tragedy after tragedy? If there is an all-powerful God, why does this suffering happen?"

At this point, many give up on God.

Our first theological response is always to hear a cry from the heart and to care about, and care for, these poor suffering ones. The second theological response is to realize that the God of Abraham is all-loving rather than all-powerful, because, for God, love is more important than power, and because love entails vulnerability.

Let me explain. Even philosophically, God is not all-powerful. There are some things that God just cannot do. For example, it is arguable that God cannot make an even greater God because God would not then be God. It is also arguable that God cannot make a square circle because circles are round. And similarly, it is arguable that God cannot give us complete freedom and, at the same time, control our decision-making, because then we would not have been given complete freedom. In giving us freedom, God gives over power.

Theologically, also, God is not all-powerful. The translations of the Bible—from Hebrew to Greek and then from Greek to Latin—wrongly suggest that our God is all-powerful. For example, the Hebrew *El Shaddai*—the "God above all gods" of Abraham—is translated into Greek as *pantokrator* or "all ruling," and then into Latin as *omnipotens* or "all powerful." The translations have changed meanings. The God of Abraham is portrayed in the Bible as a loving, caring, and vulnerable God who treasures people and feels their pain. Even in the places in the Bible where God is portrayed as angry, vengeful, and warlike, the underlying point being made is that God *cares*.

The Book of Job, which, interestingly, is located exactly in the middle of the Old Testament, is a story about an innocent person's suffering. Job is a good and wealthy man who is devoted to God. Suddenly, he suffers a terrible debilitating disease. He loses his house, his property, and his family. Some "comforters" say that Job must have done something wrong, and that God is punishing him. Job refuses to accept that his fate is punishment from God, or that God deals in punishment. Instead, extraordinarily, he continues to hope in God's friendship and love. In the end, he comes to see that the Lord God is way beyond his measure, and he finds his life restored.

In other words, the message of Job is that we do not know why God allows suffering, but Job knows God and understands that God is beyond his comprehension. While it may be true that our minds are too small, this is of little comfort to our suffering.

But what if God suffers too? What if God is crucified? We know that Jesus suffered rejection, treachery, abandonment, imprisonment, mockery, torture, trial, and crucifixion. Some say that Jesus takes on this suffering to atone for our sins, thus reconciling us to God. It is then suggested that when we suffer, we should think of Jesus and make an offering of our suffering to God. This theology of suffering, however, looks more like a transaction of debts than an act of love.

While a theology of sacrifice and atonement is part of the history of our faith, a deeper theology unfolds the profound connection between love and suffering. Instead of thinking of God as a distant God who counts debts and observes our suffering from afar, Christians are challenged to believe in a close God who is nearer to our suffering than we are, and who feels suffering just as we do. The true sacrifice is self-giving in love.

The Gospels make the point that human suffering is God's greatest concern, not strength, power, or control. Just as loving parents give their children freedom and suffer with their children, so also a loving God who gives us life and freedom is caught up in suffering when we suffer.

Loving is more about giving than receiving. To love another person means to give of oneself. In complete loving, we give everything until we have nothing left. And so, in this line of thought, infinite loving is infinite self-giving, infinite vulnerability, and an infinite embrace of suffering.

The real tricky question to ask, then, is not about God being all-powerful. Rather, the question becomes, "If God's *love* is so great, why do we suffer?"

If our sufferings occur because we have a limited physical body and we feel things, what difference can God's love make? Sometimes our suffering is a sign of care: the burnt finger saves us from burning our whole hand. We suffer hunger and thirst because our body needs food. We suffer because we have feelings, because we care about the ones we love. We could be robots, of course, and then we wouldn't feel a thing. But most of us prefer to experience feelings rather than not. The downside of being a robot is that we would not feel joy and laughter and love. So, we need to give thanks for our bodies and feelings, and be compassionate, caring, and healing when people are suffering. At this level, we might have to learn to accept our own suffering as part of the gift of life.

Perhaps God should have created a different kind of world, one in which we have no feelings, no consciousness, no freedom, no love, and no pain. This would be a loveless void. We might as well be a rock or a moon. Christians believe God is vulnerable in love and with us in pain. We find our way to God through love and pain, believing God is with us.

The tricky question now becomes, *Where is an all-loving God in this suffering?* One possible answer is that God is already there with us, feeling with us, comforting us, trying to heal us. As we move into an unknown future, with all its risk and suffering, we believe God is walking beside us into a future that is still unfolding.

The biggest pain of being human is that our lifetime is limited. We might live for ten, fifty, or one hundred years, but we will all die. We are not infinite. We are not gods. We discover this reality at every stage of life. We call it suffering. It is also limitation. In the moment of death, however, our lives become unlimited, for we are free of our physical bodies, free of being in time.

If the universe is a random event and death is the end of life, then suffering is indeed pointless and intolerable. But if our lives are part of a loved creation, and if death is not the end of our being, then suffering is quite a different concern. This does not mean that we should silently put up with suffering like the Stoics or try to transcend or deny suffering. It does not mean that God does bad things so that good things can follow. It does not mean that God is a sadist who enjoys watching us suffer. Rather, we believe that God is suffering with us as we move to the fullness of being. God feels this suffering with us. We, like God, are left vulnerable. We hope and trust that, in the end, God is with us and infinite love cannot be defeated. In our death, we come to the fullness of life. In the moment of death, my life is both complete and unlimited.

These are deep mysteries, but they are not meaningless mysteries. They relate to our next question about whether God cares about us. Does God have a plan for you and me?

10

DOES GOD HAVE A PLAN FOR ME?

Does God have a plan for me? Does God know my future? And if God does know my future, is my future already determined? And if my future is determined, what's the point of life? Great questions!

Our lives do have a purpose. We are meant to be who we are meant to be! This sounds like a cliché, but it is true. Each of us is completely unique, with a unique DNA and unique thumbprints. Even identical twins do not have identical fingerprints. Who we are and who we're meant to be unfold as we move forward on life's journey.

But does God have a plan for me? Some say that God knows everything, and that God has a book in which our future is carefully detailed and determined. In this view, God has written down our every move long before it happens. They might quote Psalm 139 to support this view:

> In your book were written
> all the days that were formed for me,
> when none of them as yet existed.
>
> (Ps 139:16)

Elsewhere in the Bible, however, the promises are more general. For example, the Lord tells Jeremiah, "I know the plans I have for you...plans for your welfare and not for harm, to give you a future with hope" (Jer 29:11). The *Catechism* recognizes that God has a plan, but describes this plan in very general terms by referring to Paul's letter to the Ephesians: the plan is "to unite all things in him" (§772).

I believe that God does have a plan for me, but it is a general plan. God's plan is that I will live my life to the full, be who I am meant to be, and be united with all creatures and creation in God's love. This is not a detailed plan where every move and every event is perfectly described before they happen. I am free to make choices.

But does God know my future? It is possible to imagine God knowing all possible futures, just as a computer playing chess can know all possible future moves and their consequences. However, this makes God seem like a remote geek, playing vapid computer games, rather than a loving Creator who walks beside me and delights in giving freedom.

It is more helpful to reflect on the powers of God and the nature of what *future* means. For example, as noted in the previous chapter, there are some things that God, by definition, cannot do: if a circle, by definition, is round, then this suggests that it would be impossible for God to create a circle with corners. Similarly, if futures that depend on free choices are unknown until those choices are made, then perhaps God cannot know our future until after we make our choices.

In my imagination, we move into the future with God beside us, as if we were unrolling a carpet that we step forward on together. God can guide and anticipate our steps, and anticipate the consequences of our actions, but the choices are left to us. That is the gift of God's love. In this way, our future is partly known and partly guided, but never determined.

Furthermore, when thinking about God's plan, and whether God knows my future, there are questions about the nature of time and the direction of time that we might consider. It is odd, for example, that we can go backward and forward in space, but not do so in time. And there are very interesting issues in physics about the relativity of time and space and the fundamental entanglement of matter at the quantum level. Perhaps God is the kind of being who can both allow for freedom and still know us intimately. Perhaps God sees the whole of time all at once, rather than sequentially as we do, with our worries about unknown futures.

So, does my life have a purpose? In previous chapters, we have talked about the difference between the scientific and biblical accounts of Creation, where one tells us *how* the universe came into being and the other tells us *why* the universe was created. If there is no purpose and meaning behind the universe, then indeed life may have no purpose.

The realization that life might be a meaningless random accident has led to considerable pessimism, but also to some admirable humanism. It is quite awesome that humanist atheists are working to build compassionate communities and just societies, developing nonreligious spirituality and altruistic services. They assert a value and dignity in life and nature.

Christians also assert a value and dignity of life and nature. We believe that the universe exists for a purpose. We were created by God out of love; each of us is a unique expression of divine love. Our purpose is to discover the truth of this being and to be who we are meant to be. I am meant to become truly myself, wholly myself. If I do this, I will ultimately be united in God's love. Being whole is also being holy. As the Bible often reminds us, God wants us to "be holy, for I am holy" (Lev 11:44–45; see also 1 Pet 1:15–16).

A CONCLUDING UNSCIENTIFIC POSTSCRIPT

Mathematically, I could win a lottery if I bought a ticket for every possible numerical combination, but that would mean buying hundreds of millions of tickets. Statistically, if I put an almost infinite number of monkeys in a room and gave each monkey a laptop computer, it is possible that in an almost infinite number of years, one monkey could randomly but accurately type out the complete works of Shakespeare. The odds are long, but it is statistically possible.

So also, it is statistically possible that a random and accidental universe could seem to have a fine-tuned design and conscious purpose. According to the big bang theory—see chapter 7—universes can erupt out of nowhere. There could be an almost infinite number of parallel universes, each with its own variations. We can never know these other universes because they have no connection with our own. Our universe just happens to be one that has coherence, just as one monkey happens to type the whole of Shakespeare. How do we explain this?

Scientifically, it is a coherent theory. Atheist scientists rightly argue that it is more reasonable to postulate an almost infinite number of universes than it is to postulate that there is a loving God who created our universe...and any other universes for that matter. Christians, however, have a deeper imagination of the richness of being.

In one episode of the TV series *The Big Bang Theory*, there is some deeper imagining between the physicists Sheldon and Leonard:

SHELDON: You know it just occurred to me, if there are an infinite number of parallel universes, in one of them there's probably a Sheldon who doesn't believe parallel universes exist.

LEONARD: Probably. What's your point?

SHELDON: No point. It's just one of those things that makes one of the *mes* chuckle.

For Christians, there is a point: there is an incomprehensible secret to all the universes, and we call this secret "God." And perhaps God chuckles, too.

11

CAN WE PROVE THE EXISTENCE OF GOD?

A few years ago, the big red London buses carried advertising, sponsored by some atheists, that read, "There's probably no God. Now stop worrying and enjoy life." Logically, however, this statement also implies, "There possibly is a God. Be not afraid and live life to the full."

Degree of difficulty warning: this chapter is not about advertising slogans, nor primarily about faith, but about arguments and proofs. There are three main kinds of proofs: first, those based on observation and experimentation; second, those based on definitions and logic; and third, those based on a mix of experience and logic.

The first kind of proofs, like scientific proofs based on experimental evidence, is called "inductive" or *a posteriori* proofs because they argue *from particular observations to a general conclusion.* For example, people in Europe noted that every swan they observed was white. From these particular observations, they reached the general conclusion that all swans were white. This was proven untrue when Europeans observed black swans in Australia. All proofs based on observation are open to revision, including scientific truths. Generally, however, new scientific theories, in one way or another, include the old observations but give a higher picture. Today, we might say all swans are either white or black, so the original claim was at least half true...until we see a blue swan on another planet in another solar system!

If it is difficult to claim absolute scientific truth from observations and experiments, in one sense it must be even more difficult to prove the existence of God from observation and experience. Even though some of us might have a personal experience of God, these experiences are not publicly accessible. They may be indicators for consideration, but they are not perfect proofs.

The second kind of proofs is based on definitions and logic. For example, if a circle is defined as the loci of all points equidistant from a given point, then it follows that the diameter is twice the length of the radius and that all the radii are of equal length. These proofs argue *from a general statement to a particular conclusion* and are called "deductive" or *a priori* proofs. The classic form of a logical proof is called a syllogism. For example:

> All squares have four sides.
> This is a square.
> Therefore, it has four sides.

These logical proofs are quite solid if you accept the starting definition, but they can be more theoretically based than based in reality. A more complicated classical syllogism, starting with a definition based on experience, is

> All men are mortal.
> Socrates is a man.
> Therefore, Socrates is mortal.

There are several proofs for the existence of God of this kind, sometimes referred to as the five ways of St. Thomas Aquinas. For example, there is the argument from causality that we have noted above:

> Everything we see has a cause and is not the cause of itself.
> But this causal chain cannot be infinitely long.
> Therefore, there must be an uncaused cause, which we call God.

This argument is persuasive, but it is also open to three reasonable critiques: first, the idea of "causality" is difficult to prove with absolute certainty; second, it is possible that the causal chain could be infinitely long, or circular; and third, physics suggests that the universe does not need a cause and can explain its own existence.

There is an earlier logical proof, attributed to St. Anselm and called the Ontological Argument, which dazzles our minds. It states,

> God is the greatest of all beings, and nothing greater than God can exist.
> A being that exists in reality is greater than a being that exists only in the
>   imagination.
> Therefore, God must exist in reality.

Philosophers argue for and against this argument. I'm still not sure!

However, there is a third set of proofs, called transcendental arguments, that combines scientific experience with philosophical logic. In a transcendental argument, we reflect on our experience, and, in particular, we reflect on the implications (or necessary conditions) for having that experience. For example, Descartes's famous argument "I think therefore I am" is a form of transcendental argument:

I experience myself as thinking.

In order to think, it is necessary to exist.

Therefore, I exist.

There are various transcendental arguments for the existence of God. A modest transcendental argument for the existence of God has to do with our experience of human limitation. This is best explained by putting an elaborate old key on the table and asking, "What does this key disclose to us?" The usual response is "There is a lock somewhere that it can open." And then we can ask, "And does this key tell us the exact inside shape of this lock?" And the correct answer is "Yes, the lock has to be of such a shape that the key will exactly fit it." And so, even though we cannot see the lock, and even though the lock may not exist, we know what the lock will look like.

We can also think of a human being as a key that does not explain its own existence. Our human yearning poses the questions, "What is missing here?" and "What does the mystery of human existence disclose to us?" And the answer would be infinite love, infinite meaning, infinite compassion, infinite fidelity. In other words, our experience of being finite and seeking complete love discloses the possibility of a being that explains its own existence, a being of infinite love.

This argument doesn't say that such a God necessarily exists. It argues that our experience of being limited and yet desiring more discloses the possibility of unlimited being—just as a key discloses a keyhole. It discloses what a God for us would be like. Some might say that this argument suggests that we make God according to our needs and image. The reverse is also true because it suggests a God that transcends our own limitation, a God who is infinite and universal. This God is not an idol in our image, but a God beyond idols.

All these proofs for God, even if they are effective, fall short of telling us very much about God. The philosophical arguments produce a God we can *think* about, rather than the *living* God of Abraham, a God who wants to be close to us. The Catholic

Church wisely teaches that there are "so called proofs for the existence of God, not in the sense of proofs in the natural sciences, but rather in the sense of 'converging and convincing arguments,' which allow us to attain certainty about the truth" (*Catechism* 31).

Richard Dawkins, who promoted that advertisement on the London buses, considers the arguments of "theologians who take seriously the possibility that God does not exist and argue that he does." He raises much the same concerns about these arguments as we have noted already. Dawkins then concludes that "there is almost certainly no God."[1] However, his argument for "why there is almost certainly no God" is far from certain. It starts with a critique of the "first cause" or "designer" argument and then develops like this:

> Only the existence of God can explain the complex improbable appearance of design in the universe.
>
> The designer hypothesis immediately raises the larger problem of who designed the designer.
>
> This is an infinite regress (a self-defeating skyhook hypothesis) and science can offer a better explanation (even though physics cannot yet offer us a strongly satisfying explanation).[2]

The argument is sound if you define God as designer and define all design as needing explanation. But there are two major flaws here. First, the definition of God as "designer" is limited, because, for most believers, God is experienced in relational and existential ways rather than as a designer. Second, if God is defined as a being, which is its own explanation, rather than as a designer, then the rest of the argument fails. Dawkins, with some justification, argues against Anselm's ontological argument, if perhaps rather sarcastically, and he would no doubt argue against the reality of the idea of a being that is its own explanation. This does not, however, convince me that "there is almost certainly no God."

In fact, we can only attain certainty about the truth if we encounter God in our lives rather than just in our philosophy. We can meet God in prayer, revelations, love, mystical experiences, but can we possibly encounter God as an earthling? That really

---

1. Richard Dawkins, *The God Delusion*, paperback ed. (London: Black Swan, 2007), 14, chaps. 3 and 4.
2. Dawkins, *The God Delusion*, 14, 188–89.

would be something. This brings us to the Gospels and the story of Jesus of Nazareth, which we discuss in the next chapter.

Black holes, by definition, cannot be observed because they reflect no light. When we see stars moving in tight circles around some central point, we suspect there is a strong gravitational force pulling at them. But we can see nothing at this center point. We infer that there might be a black hole there, where the gravitational force is so strong that not even light can escape its pull. Perhaps one day, scientists will see a kind of shadow at this center point that further indicates the presence of a black hole.

Proofs for the existence of God are similar, though even more demanding. Like a black hole, God is unobservable because God is not a thing. But just as we can see signs in the universe that suggest the existence of black holes, so we can also see signs in both creation and our own lives that suggest that God might be at the heart of all being, explaining why we exist and for whom we exist.

12

WHAT IS THE DIFFERENCE BETWEEN JESUS AND GOD?

We read in the Gospels that Jesus was born in a stable in Bethlehem. Mary was his mother and Joseph his foster father. He grew up in Nazareth and became a carpenter. We learn that Jesus gets hungry and thirsty. He weeps and embraces. He bleeds and dies. All this evidence suggests that he was truly human, just like us. Indeed, in our culture today, Jesus is loved as a cool guy: free, gentle, inspiring, brave, speaking truth to power, and caring for the excluded. So why do we treat him as God?

The answer is that in the same Scripture, we read that Jesus's first companions came to see him first as the Messiah, and then as the same as God. For example:

> "'Look, the virgin shall conceive and bear a son, and they shall name him Emmanuel,' which means, 'God is with us'" (Matt 1:23).

> "For in him the whole fullness of deity dwells bodily" (Col 2:9).

> "In the beginning was the Word, and the Word was with God, and the Word was God. He was in the beginning with God" (John 1:1–3).

> "The Father and I are one" (John 10:30).

> "Whoever has seen me has seen the Father" (John 14:9).

Such texts suggest that Jesus was more than a very cool guy. The early Christians' accounts of Jesus's birth, miracles, teaching, death, and resurrection all suggest superhuman characteristics: Jesus's love is absolute, infinite, and unconditional; Jesus's closeness to God is so intimate that the two are almost one. Jesus is indeed cool and awesome, but to such an extreme that—unlike pop stars who come and go—his identity is both human and divine.

This seems impossible. How could Jesus be both human and divine when humans are limited, and God is unlimited? What is the difference between Jesus and God? How can someone who is clearly human also be divine?

These questions were raised in the first centuries of the Church, especially among the Greek-speaking communities. Some Christians—called Docetists—argued that Jesus was purely divine. He only played the role of being human rather than being fully human. Others—called Arians—argued that Jesus was human, and a holy man, but not divine.

These were both "either/or" arguments that were influenced by the logic and reasoning of the Greek philosophers. The first great council of the Church, the Council of Nicaea (325), agreed on a broader view of reality and rejected the Arian views. The Father and the Son were declared to be of the same divine substance, and Jesus was declared to be both fully human and fully divine. For the council, "both/and" expresses a higher view of reality than "either/or." But how can this be explained?

Things can be different and the same. First, and most obviously, there are physical differences in shape and size and color. For example, a banana is different from an apple. The apple is red, round, and crisp; the banana is yellow, cylindrical, and soft. But bananas and apples are both fruits; they are thus the same and different. There can also be differences through naming: your hat might be identical to my hat, except that mine is mine and yours is yours; but if you look inside my hat, you will see it has my name on it. So, the hats are both the same and different.

There can be differences of relationship: my mother is also someone's sister and someone's daughter and someone's aunt. My mother is the same, but to each of her relatives, she is different. There can be differences regarding the deep-down essence or nature or substance of something. For example, two people might be completely different in their appearance, their height, their weight, their gender, their nationality, their age, their language, their clothes, and so on. They may be different, but they are both human.

Jesus and the God of Abraham seem to differ in relationship: Jesus calls himself "Son" and he calls God "Abba/Father." Jesus and the God of Abraham seem to differ physically: the disciples could see and touch Jesus, whereas the God of Abraham, while close, is elusive. One is immanent, the other transcendent. Jesus and the God of Abraham differ in name: one is called the Christ; the other is called God. For all these differences, however, deep down their divine essence (nature or substance) is the same. Just as we are all human, Jesus and the Lord God are both divine. That's why the Church decided to clarify the conundrum by declaring in the Nicene Creed that

Jesus was "consubstantial with the Father." In other words, while they were different in many respects, they were, in essence, the same.

This explanation raises another problem, however, because if Jesus is divine and Abba Father is divine, doesn't that imply there are two Gods? The Bible, however, tells us very clearly there is only one God. For example: "The LORD is God in heaven above and on the earth beneath; there is no other" (Deut 4:39). And logically, if there were two Gods, then each would be limited by the other, and neither would be fully God. This conundrum was addressed by the Council of Bishops at Chalcedon in the year 451, which declared that Jesus, while one person, was both fully human and fully divine. Jesus and God are different as "persons" but the same as divine. In the next chapter, we explore this idea that the fullness of the one God is not a single isolated person but a community of persons in relationship.

It takes a large mind to embrace the possibility that Jesus is both fully human and fully divine. Some might say it seems illogical and, therefore, nonsense. A clever student might appeal to my earlier argument about suffering and God's power, where I argued that God's power is limited in that God cannot do something that, by definition, is impossible; for example, making a square round. But is it impossible, by definition, for a human to be divine or for the divine to be human? If we regard the human as being primarily a collection of atoms, then this might be the case, because God cannot be limited to material reality. However, if we define the essence of being human as being unconditionally open to love, and if we define the divine as infinite love, then arguably the human and the divine are two aspects of infinite love.

Both contemporary philosophy and contemporary physics make it clear that, as things become more complex, we need more than one word to describe reality. Contemporary philosophy, sometimes called postmodernism, reminds us that there is no precise connection necessarily between a word and a thing. And in contemporary physics, as noted in an earlier chapter, we find something even more dramatic: we need to use opposing words to capture the full reality of things beyond our ordinary experience. For example, an electron is only fully understood if it is described as both a wave and a particle, even though, in many ways, a wave is the very opposite of a particle. Jesus is a complex reality and can only be fully described by using apparently opposite terms.

Therefore, we should expect nothing less of the God of love than that God would want to be fully with us. If somebody loved you, wouldn't you want them to show they care about you? They could perhaps send a card or call you by phone. Best of all, however, would be if they took the trouble to come and visit you and show their love.

Similarly, surely a God who is truly loving and caring about creation would want to be intimately involved in creation, not just be a remote, uncaring, distant observer. It makes sense that God, to do this fully—and God, by definition, does not do things by halves—would become flesh, as Scripture says, or "incarnate," as the Latin is translated into English.

The awesome consequence of the theology of the incarnation is not just that the divine becomes human, but also that *the human has the capacity to bear the divine.* The life that Jesus models for us is the fullness of human life—divine life—and this is ultimately why Jesus is so "cool." Being truly human has divine potential.

The *Catechism* summarizes its teaching on the human and divine natures of Christ as follows:

> Jesus Christ is true God and true man, in the unity of his divine person; for this reason, he is the one and only mediator between God and men.
>
> Jesus Christ possesses two natures, one divine and the other human, not confused, but united in the one person of God's Son.
>
> Christ, being true God and true man, has a human intellect and will, perfectly attuned and subject to his divine intellect and divine will, which he has in common with the Father and the Holy Spirit.
>
> The Incarnation is therefore the mystery of the wonderful union of the divine and human natures in the one person of the Word. (§§480–83)

These rather clinical statements clarify the Church's understanding of the relationship between Jesus and God. The Gospels, however, invite us to walk with the disciples, learning from Jesus and watching his ways. Eventually, like the disciples on the road to Emmaus after the crucifixion and resurrection, our eyes are opened and we see Jesus for who he really is.

13

HOW CAN GOD BE ONE AND THREE? WHO IS THE HOLY SPIRIT?

So, there is a story about a holy man walking along the beach at sunrise. He is thinking about God and trying to comprehend how God can be present and yet elusive, and how God can be one and three. Then looking ahead, he sees a child playing on the shore. The child digs a hole in the sand with a big shell, goes to the sea and fills the shell with water, and then tips the water from the shell into the hole. "What are you doing?" asks the holy man. The child replied, "I'm putting the ocean into this hole I've dug." "But you can't pour the whole of the ocean into that small hole," said the holy man. "Nor can you fit the whole of God into your small brain," said the child.

The holy man was St. Augustine. The child was directly or indirectly a messenger of God.

Nonetheless, the question of how God can be one God and three persons, as Christians have constantly believed, still calls for a reasonable response.

A common explanation is to point to examples where one is also three. Consider water. Most of us first experience water as a liquid. Then, we discover ice cubes as frozen water, and we discover steam as water turns to gas. The three appearances are different, but underneath they are differing arrangements of the same molecule. Ice is neither liquid water nor steam. Steam is neither ice nor liquid water. Yet all three are H_2O.

The early Christian community experienced God in three ways. They experienced God as a transcendent Creator, they experienced the Spirit of God as moving through creation and guiding them, and they experienced Jesus Christ as being born through the power of the Spirit and walking among us. The Father is not the Spirit, the Spirit is not the Son, and the Son is not the Father; yet each is fully God.

Let us consider the Bible's account of these experiences in greater detail. The opening words of the Bible tell us that "in the beginning when God created the heavens and the earth, the earth was a formless void and darkness covered the face of the deep, while a wind [the spirit] from God swept over the face of the waters" (Gen 1:1–2). Similarly, the Prophet Isaiah speaks of the Spirit of the Lord resting on a savior who is to come: "A shoot shall come out from the stump of Jesse, and a branch shall grow out of his roots. The spirit of the LORD shall rest on him" (Isa 11:1–2). Here the Spirit is understood to be God's power and agency. We can read many accounts of the Spirit of God in the Jewish Scriptures.

In the Christian Scriptures, we read of the Holy Spirit "coming upon" Mary the mother of Jesus. The same Spirit later drives Jesus into the desert, descends on Jesus at his baptism, and is promised to his disciples after his death: "You will receive power when the Holy Spirit has come upon you" (Acts 1:8). The Acts of the Apostles then tells the story of the Holy Spirit inspiring the disciples at Pentecost. In the New Testament, this Spirit is variously called the Spirit of Jesus, or the Spirit of God, or the Spirit of the Holy, or the Advocate. This Spirit is described as the Spirit of God as well as the Spirit of Jesus's power and agency.

In the previous chapter, we discussed the relationship between Jesus and the Father. The early Christians thus came to believe there were intimate links among the three names for God: between God the Father and the Son, and between God the Father and the Holy Spirit, and between Jesus and the Holy Spirit. The belief was that God is a trinity, a community of three, rather than a monolith. If God is love, then it makes sense that the Trinity is a community of love.

We know that this trinitarian view was held very early in the first Christian communities because of the way St. Paul greeted the Corinthians in one of his letters: "The grace of the Lord Jesus Christ, the love of God, and the communion of the Holy Spirit be with all of you" (2 Cor 13:13). Similarly, by the time the Gospel of Matthew was completed, somewhere in the second half of the first century, Christians were being baptized with our familiar trinitarian formula: "In the name of the Father and of the Son and of the Holy Spirit" (Matt 28:19).

Given these very early beliefs, that the divine seemed to have three different names or functions, it didn't take long for the more philosophically minded Greek Christians to ask how there could be only one God. This issue was connected to the paradox about the humanity and divinity of Christ, which was resolved at the Council of Nicaea, as discussed in the previous chapter. The early theologians proposed that while each of the three members of the Trinity was believed to be fully God, they could, at the same time, be understood as distinctly different "persons."

The original Greek word for *person* is *prosopon*, which is the word for the mask or face put on by an actor in a play to highlight their identity and role. In this way, one actor could play three distinct roles by wearing three different masks. The problem with this analogy, however, is that it might suggest the three persons in the Trinity are only one person playing three roles. This is not what Christians believe, and it is not what the Church intends to teach.

The formal teachings and traditions of the Church about the Trinity are essentially that the Father is fully God, and the Son is fully God, and the Spirit is fully God, but the Father is not the Son, and the Son is not the Spirit, and the Spirit is not the Father. They are different as persons but singular as God.

In other words, we experience God in three ways:

1. When we wonder at nature, or wonder at our own existence, we experience God as mysterious and hidden, and yet also present and personal. We use some pointing words and call this God "Father and Creator." This is not to say that God is male or patriarchal, but rather that God is personal and that God cares. This transcendent God holds all creation in love and is fully God.

2. When we hear the gospel, celebrate the Eucharist, love our neighbor, serve the poor, and heal the sick, we encounter Jesus Christ, who is truly human and who walked among us, and who showed the face of the one he called "Abba Father." This incarnate or immanent God shows perfect infinite love and is, therefore, fully God.

3. Sometimes we sense that God is engaging us in our spiritual senses,[1] particularly when we are trying to follow the way of Jesus and are gathered in Christian work and Christian community. We experience a personal call and personal guidance. This is not just a vague emotion, but an invitation from God. This presence is personal and has a name. We call this the Holy Spirit, the Spirit of God, and the Spirit of Jesus. Because God cannot do things by halves, the Spirit of God is fully God.

These deeper explanations of the Trinity may require stretching our small brain. If we limit ourselves to an old scientific view of reality, we may struggle to give

---

1. See chapter 8 for more on this concept of the spiritual senses.

primary importance to concepts like "love," "person," and "community." In contemporary physics, however, our attention has shifted from individual "things" in space and time, like atoms and molecules, to the forces and energies that hold things together and that extend throughout space and time. Perhaps the "connections" are more important than the individual "things." Perhaps God is best understood as perfect "love," which involves persons, rather than as an individual; as "being" rather than as "a being."

There are different ways of understanding identity and reality. In Australian Aboriginal communities, for example, the identity or spirit of a person is often linked with the spirit of the place where they were conceived. Many groups identify themselves with specific birds or animals that live in the place of their birth. For example, there is the story of two little boys playing together when the smaller of the boys suddenly started crying in pain. It turned out the bigger boy was throwing sticks at a goanna lizard in a tree. This goanna, however, happened to be the younger boy's "totem" (as the anthropologists would say). For the little boy, an attack on the goanna was as painful as an attack on himself. While he and the goanna were different, he and the goanna were also one. That was the way he saw the world. His individuality was linked with the whole community of nature. This deeper view of reality gave a richer understanding of belonging and identity.

Several theologians, starting with St. Gregory of Nazianzus in the fourth century, have argued that we might think of God as an interpersonal community of love, an interpersonal community of complete giving and receiving. They used the word *perichoresis*, which is related to our word *choreography*, and means "dancing together." The intended meaning is that God is the most intimate of dances, a co-inherence with each other. We are invited to be dancers in this dance.

This theology of the Trinity is appealing, but it can become complex. For practical Christians today, it is difficult to distinguish between Father, Son, and Spirit, especially when we live in the age of the Spirit. Perhaps it is best to focus on Jesus Christ as the image of the unseen God whose Spirit is with us here and now, and then drift into the mystery of the unseen God.

One final question might be raised here about the English words we use for the Trinity: *Father, Son,* and *Holy Spirit.* These words are enshrined in our faith, but they are pointing words, and they differ from language to language. The English words themselves are not sacrosanct. In my own lifetime, the Church has made a fundamental change to the trinitarian formula. When I was young, we blessed ourselves in the name of "the Father, the Son, and *the Holy Ghost.*" The word *ghost* was eventually seen to be misleading. It was replaced by *Spirit*, which is indeed a better translation of the earlier Greek and Latin words.

Expressions of faith can change, as noted in chapter 4. It is a big step, however, to change the words *Father* and *Son*—even though they are pointing words rather than exact names, even though they are translations rather than originals, and even though they are gendered words and inappropriate, given that God does not have a gender. The words we currently use are also important because they describe *relationships* within the Trinity, rather than *functions*. In the Creeds, nonetheless, we do speak of God the Father as also being "Creator of heaven and earth," the Son as the one who came "for our salvation," and the Holy Spirit as "the giver of life." Perhaps we can bless ourselves "in the name of the Father our Creator, and of the Son our Savior, and of the Holy Spirit who gives us Life," or using some variation.

Whatever words we use for God will always fall short. A wordless Sign of the Cross is perhaps more profound. In Christian faith, we sometimes talk about seeing the face of God after we have died, or seeing God "as he is" (1 John 3:2). This is called the "beatific vision." Karl Rahner notes, however, that the beatific vision is not so much that we see and comprehend God for the first time, but rather that we see and comprehend the full wonder of the *incomprehensibility* of God for the first time. After many years of writing about God, one of Rahner's final essays was "The Inexhaustible Transcendence of God,"[2] where he reminds us again that God is "ineffable," meaning that, in the end, we can say nothing about the utter transcendence of God.

The child by the seashore indeed offered us good advice: "Nor can you fit the whole of God into your small brain."

---

2. Karl Rahner, "The Inexhaustible Transcendence of God and Our Concern for the Future," in *Concern for the Church*, Theological Investigations, vol. 20 (New York: Crossroad Publishing, 1981), 173–86.

14

IS GOD THE SAME IN ALL RELIGIONS? WHY IS OUR GOD THE TRUE GOD?

These are two good questions. The answer to the first question is yes, no, and maybe. First, there are a few world religions, known as Abrahamic religions, that arose in the Middle East and believe the God of Abraham to be the one true God. These include Judaism, Christianity, and Islam, as well as the more local Samaritan, Bahai, Bayani, Kurdish, Mandean, Druze, and Rastafari religions. Within each of these Abrahamic religions, however, and across all these religions, there are varying understandings of God and differing teachings and practices.

Second, there are many world religions that originate from South Asia, most notably Hinduism and Buddhism and their antecedents. Hinduism has a long history and unclear origins, though it probably developed from related local religions and a subsequent collection of Vedic hymns. While, on the one hand, there are many Gods in Hinduism—some say 330 million—on the other hand, these Gods can be understood as representations of Brahman, who pervades the entire universe. Brahman is the supreme Spirit and, therefore, the one true God. Jainism and Sikhism hold some beliefs in common with Hinduism.

Interestingly, some scholars argue that the story of Brahman and his consort, Sarasvati, must relate to the story of Abraham and his wife, Sarah, given the similarity in their names. Others argue that Brahman and Abraham have their origins in the Egyptian God called Ra. Brahman may differ in many respects from the God of Abraham, but both traditions depict a God who is personal and above all beings.

Buddhism, which grew out of Hinduism, has a variety of forms. Initially, the focus in Buddhism seems less on God and more on the self. This kind of nontheism may rightly be the rejection of a domesticated God rather than the rejection of a transcendent God. There are some forms of Buddhism that directly or indirectly support the idea of an eternal, all-pervading, uncreated Ground of Being. Such an idea of God seems not far removed from the incomprehensibility of God discussed in the previous chapter.

Third, there is another group of East Asian religions—most notably Taoism, Confucianism, and Shinto—with hundreds of millions of followers. Here, there is a common emphasis on the Tao as a guide to life, but often with ritual offerings and prayers to a pantheon of gods and spirits.

Finally, there are also hundreds, if not thousands, of local or tribal cultures that have quite different ways of shaping what a Western mind might regard as a religion. For these peoples, there is no distinction between the sacred and the profane, given that spirit is present in all aspects of life. Some local religions may have idols and sacrifices and prayers; others may have neither prayer nor sacrifice yet celebrate the presence of the creator spirit in all aspects of their life.

Some philosophers have argued that humans, in their desire for meaning, create a God in their own image. Perhaps this explains why God is in many ways seen to be the same in all religions: personal, creator, transcendent, spirit, omnipresent, benevolent, one, loving, and the highest of all being. It is equally arguable, however, that God is seen to be quite different in various religions, whether as Trinity in Christian faith or as Rainbow Serpent in Australian Aboriginal Dreaming. In other words, we humans do not entirely make God in our own image.

Theologically, if we believe that there is a God who is personal, creator, transcendent, spirit, omnipresent, benevolent, one, loving, and the highest of all beings, then there can only be one such God. It follows that the different accounts of God across all religions are either equally false or, more subtly, that they equally express different facets of the one God rather than several different Gods. After all, we do not have the capacity to comprehend the whole of God. Philosophically, it could be argued that God is the same in all religions, but that each religion celebrates different facets of God.

For Christians, however, Jesus Christ is believed to show the face of the one true God, uniquely and completely. Then comes the really tricky question: *What right do Christians have to think that our God is the one true God, and that all the other religions and Gods are only second rate?*

First, Christians understand God to be for all peoples, not just for themselves; and second, we understand other religions to have arisen from a shared sense of the great spirit at the heart of creation and at the heart of human beings. We believe this universal sense of a transcendent God is an invitation into a relationship that God gives to every human being. This is not part of human nature so much as a gift freely given or a grace that God offers to all human beings. Some religions respond to this invitation by giving God specific names and qualities. Others respect the absolute mystery of God. Our belief is that God's covenant with Abraham and God's incarnation in Jesus deepen the relationships between God and all humankind, as well as between God and all creation. Furthermore, if the revelation in Jesus Christ is in one sense complete and total—a once-and-for-all event—then the Abraham story and the Jesus event help us make sense of all religions, rather than exclude all religions.

Nevertheless, Catholics should be very humble about making these exalted claims. Groucho Marx of the Marx Brothers, after being asked why he wanted to resign from an elite club, wrote, "I don't want to belong to any club that would accept me as a member." Taking a similar stance, I would not want to belong to any faith community that thought it had exclusive rights on God, because God's love must be unbounded, and God needs to be unbounded. God is not our possession. If we go back to both Scripture and Church teaching, the foundations of our simple theology, we find that there are both exclusive and inclusive claims on God in our faith tradition.

The exclusive claims come as part of the fundamental covenant between the God of Abraham and the descendants of Abraham. For example, the Ten Commandments begin, "I am the Lord your God, who brought you out of the land of Egypt, out of the house of slavery; you shall have no other gods before me" (Exod 20:2–3). Alongside this view, however, the Jewish Scriptures are full of universal claims for God, starting with the Lord God's words to Abraham: "In you all the families of the earth shall be blessed" (Gen 12:3). The story of Jonah and the unbelieving people of Nineveh further illustrates this abiding belief that the God of Abraham is also a God for all peoples.

The Christian Scriptures tell a similar story, with a clear preference for inclusion of all peoples and all faiths. When Jesus talks with the Samaritan woman at the well, she asks him whether God is to be found on the holy mountain in Samaria or in the Temple in Jerusalem. Jesus's answer suggests that we need to recognize that God transcends any place of worship, because "the hour is coming…when the true worshipers will worship the Father in spirit and truth" (John 4:23). When St. Paul is debating the Greek philosophers about God, he explains that there is only one God who made the world and is close to each one of us:

> The God who made the world and everything in it…does not live in shrines made by human hands….From one ancestor he made all nations to inhabit

the whole earth, and he allotted the times of their existence and the boundaries of the places where they would live, so that they would search for God and perhaps grope for him and find him—though indeed he is not far from each one of us. (Acts 17:24–27)

Catholic Church teaching deeply respects other religions, and not in a condescending or patronizing way. The Church teaches that Catholics can learn about God from other religions. At the Second Vatican Council, for example, a Declaration was prepared on the relationship of the Church to non-Christian religions. Among other things, it states,

> Other religions found everywhere try to counter the restlessness of the human heart, each in its own manner, by proposing "ways," comprising teachings, rules of life, and sacred rites. The Catholic Church rejects nothing that is true and holy in these religions. She regards with sincere reverence those ways of conduct and of life, those precepts and teachings which, though differing in many aspects from the ones she holds and sets forth, nonetheless often reflect a ray of that Truth which enlightens all men. (*Nostra Aetate* 2)

Pope John Paul II, when meeting in Alice Springs with the Australian Aborigines, representatives of the oldest continuing human culture in the world, took this theology even further. He encouraged them to hold onto their own way of touching the mystery of God. He said, "Your 'Dreaming,' which influences your lives so strongly that…you remain for ever people of your culture, is your only way of touching the mystery of God's Spirit in you and in creation. You must keep your striving for God and hold on to it in your lives."[1]

Consequently, we should not think other religions are second rate. They are a response to God's invitation through creation and through the yearning of the human heart. They can teach us reverence and spirituality. Our God *is* the true God, but Jesus reveals that the God at the heart of other religions is also the true God.

So, the answers to our initial questions are these: first, Catholics believe that the one true God is at the heart of the truth and holiness of all religions; second, the one true God is, therefore, also at the heart of Christianity; third, the unique incarnation

---

1. Pope John Paul II, "To the Aborigines and Torres Strait Islanders in Blatherskite Park," Alice Springs, Australia, November 29, 1986.

of God in Jesus Christ is the complete revelation of the one true God as loving, creating, and saving.

There follows a further question about the uniqueness of Jesus. Theologians sometimes describe this as "the scandal of particularity." This, however, is a tricky question about Jesus, and perhaps a matter for another book.

15

IS GOD THE SAME AS NATURE?

Many young people speak of finding God in nature. Many speak of nourishing their spirit through the beauty of nature. Many a surfer says, "My church is the ocean." Many a mountain climber says, "I feel closest to God when I am on top of a mountain." Many a contemplative finds God in the desert. The question often arises, "Is God the same as nature?" The simple answer is, "Not quite, but almost." Much depends on what we mean by "nature."

One great gift of television is the mind-boggling documentation of the beauty of our planet and the wonder of the universe. Hosts like Brian Cox and David Attenborough speak in hushed tones of the extraordinary variety and order in the natural world. Informed by science, they offer explanations for how creatures have evolved the way they do, and how the universe has unfolded over time in spectacular variety. While not avowing any specific God, they speak with reverence and enthusiasm about the forces of nature. But what of nature itself?

There are ancient myths that personify nature as "Mother Nature," "Mother Earth," or the Greek Goddess Gaia, and this kind of usage lingers on today. It was common practice to explain natural phenomena that we did not understand by appealing to a divine power. For example, in Norse mythology, thunder and lightning were attributed to the hammer-wielding god, Thor, rather than to electrostatic forces. Where there was a gap in our knowledge of nature, then God would be invoked as an explanation. As science explained these gaps in more detail, there was less necessity to invoke this so-called God of the gaps and less need for God. Quantum theory, however, entails that there are gaps that, by their nature, we can never penetrate.

Perhaps the deepest mysteries of nature remain unsolvable. Albert Einstein is often quoted in these terms. For example:

> The most beautiful thing we can experience is the mysterious. It is the source of all true art and science. He to whom this emotion is a stranger,

who can no longer pause to wonder and stand rapt in awe, is as good as dead: his eyes are closed.[1]

Every one who is seriously involved in the pursuit of science becomes convinced that a spirit is manifest in the laws of the Universe—a spirit vastly superior to that of man, and one in the face of which we with our modest powers must feel humble.[2]

Similarly, Niels Bohr, the founder of quantum mechanics, conceded that his theory meant we could never fully describe nature:

From a deeper and deeper exploration of our basic outlook greater and greater coherence is understood and thus we come to live under an ever richer impression of an eternal and infinite harmony, although we can only feel the vague presence of this harmony but never really grasp it.[3]

While Einstein and Bohr seem to agree on some sort of mystery at the heart of nature, note that neither of them believed in a personal God or committed themselves to any religion. Einstein clarified his position thus: "I believe in Spinoza's God who reveals himself in the orderly harmony of what exists, not in a God who concerns himself with the fate and actions of human beings."[4]

Richard Dawkins, who wrote *The God Delusion* to attack fundamentalist views of God, thinks it would have been better if scientists like Einstein stopped talking about God. "I wish that physicists would refrain from using the word God in their special metaphorical sense," he wrote, because "the metaphorical or pantheist God of the physicists is light years away from...the God of the Bible." With Dawkins, I agree that the God of the Bible is different from nature as such. But against Dawkins, I would argue that the God of the Bible is also intimately present in nature.

Scientists, like Einstein and Bohr, provide credible support for the ideas of "a spirit vastly superior to that of man" and an "eternal and infinite harmony" at the

---

1. Albert Einstein, *Living Philosophies* (New York: Simon and Schuster, 1931).

2. "Letter of January 24, 1936 to a schoolgirl, Phyllis Wright," in John C. Lennox, *God and Stephen Hawking: Whose Design Is It Anyway?* (Oxford: Lion Hudson, 2011), 44. For more on Einstein's views on religion, see Max Jammer, *Einstein and Religion: Physics and Theology* (Princeton, NJ: Princeton University Press, 2002).

3. For more on Bohr's views of mysticism, see John Honner, "Niels Bohr and the mysticism of Nature," *Zygon* 17, no. 3 (1983): 243–53.

4. Baruch Spinoza was a seventeenth-century Dutch philosopher who equated God with the natural universe, seeing God as a dynamic force, an infinite independent substance from which everything else is derived.

heart of nature. Christian faith, while unproven in scientific terms, is not unreasonable in scientific terms. Christians simply take a further step, believing in the presence of the divine at the heart of the material universe. For example, St. Paul speaks of Jesus Christ who fills the universe in all its parts (see Eph 1:23). St. Irenaeus writes in the third century, "The creator of the world is truly the Word of God, and this is Our Lord...who is inherent in the entire creation." In his encyclical letter on ecology and care for our planet, *Laudato Si'*, Pope Francis writes,

> The universe unfolds in God, who fills it completely. Hence, there is a mystical meaning to be found in a leaf, in a mountain trail, in a dewdrop, in a poor person's face. The ideal is not only to pass from the exterior to the interior to discover the action of God in the soul, but also to discover God in all things. (§233)

To understand the difference between Spinoza's God and a Christian's God, we need to understand the difference between pantheism and panentheism. The word *pantheism* identifies God with the material universe. In other words, for the pantheist, God and nature are the same. This is Spinoza's and Einstein's God. Christians are not pantheists, but they could be described as "panentheist," which means that God is present in the universe yet greater than the universe. For Christians, God is primarily personal rather than the power of nature. God loves creation and cares about creation, and God's traces are found in creation. Indeed, creation can be understood as a real presence of God.

Einstein finds this faith in a personal God "naïve." However, Dawkins, on the one hand, finds the God of the Bible to be "interventionist, miracle-wreaking, thought-reading, sin-punishing, prayer-answering." On the other hand, he respects "subtle, nuanced...understated, decent, revisionist" religion.[5] The word *revisionist* suggests a rewrite or reinterpretation. A proper reading of the Bible, however, as noted in chapter 2, "should carefully investigate what meaning the sacred writers really intended, and what God wanted to manifest by means of their words." Meaning is not being revised so much as uncovered. A careful reading of the Bible suggests a subtler understanding of God than Dawkins reports.

Like Dawkins, the late great scientist Stephen Hawking, in his posthumous book, *Brief Answers to the Big Questions*, presents a narrow idea of God: outside the universe,

---

5. Richard Dawkins, *The God Delusion*, paperback ed. (London: Black Swan, 2007), 41, 15.

directing the universe, and separate from nature. Given such an understanding of God, he then can argue,

> There is no God. No one directs the universe....I prefer to think that everything can be explained another way, by the laws of nature....We are each free to believe what we want, and it's my view that the simplest explanation is that there is no God.

Teachers of religion have a lot to answer for if they teach children that God is primarily to be understood as "director of the universe" rather than as a "loving creator who is present in nature." Hawking is perhaps scientifically correct in saying that the simplest explanation for the physical universe is that there is no God. The laws of physics, almost by definition, will always offer the simplest explanations for physical observations. But do they offer an elegant explanation for human aspiration and the beauty of nature?

While belief in a personal God is an act of faith, I have argued that such faith is not unreasonable, particularly if it is guided by a careful reading of the Bible and an understanding of the findings of science. Such faith is therefore not "naïve." If it is reasonable to believe in a mystery at the heart of nature (as do both Einstein and Bohr), and to believe in evolution and different levels of being (as does Dawkins), surely it is also reasonable, even if an act of faith, to believe in the possibility of a higher being, a personal God at the heart of nature.

Further aspects of this question, particularly the notion of the Cosmic Christ and the relationship between Jesus and creation, are matters for another discussion.

16

WHY DOESN'T GOD ANSWER MY PRAYERS?

We could make a pointed joke with the student who asks this question by asking the student, "I'll answer your question if you can answer my question: Why don't students always do what *they* are asked to do?" This is a serious question, however, and it must be taken seriously.

Students know the differences between trivial and serious prayers. For example, a student knows that praying to win a race or praying to come first in an exam is probably not the sort of prayer that God is going to rush to answer, because it is self-centered. However, praying to be the best I can be might be a prayer God would answer because God wants me to be the best I can be, and this prayer is God-centered. In the light of this, there is little point in praying to be different from who I am, like praying to be smarter, funnier, bigger, or smaller. We might consider praying to be the person God made me to be, and to love myself as much as God loves me. God will answer those prayers. And, surely, when we pray for others who are innocently suffering—like a classmate with cancer or children in refugee camps—God should be interested in these prayers.

Some aspects of this question have been discussed in chapters 9 and 10, such as why God allows suffering and whether God has a plan for me. This chapter is more concerned with the power of prayer and whether God can intervene in human history.

There are many definitions of prayer and many ways of praying: sometimes we ask God for help; sometimes we thank God for help; sometimes we praise God for the wonder and beauty of nature; and sometimes we just sit close to God, silent in the presence of God, and growing in closeness to God.

We know from the Gospels that Jesus was constantly praying to his Father. When the disciples asked Jesus to teach them how to pray, he gave them the Our Father. This is a prayer that begins with praise of God and has its focus on God's will: thus, we pray "your kingdom come, your will be done" before we pray "give us this day our daily bread" and "deliver us from evil."

But does God answer our prayers? Our Scriptures are ambiguous. We read that the Lord will hear the cry of the poor, save the crushed in spirit, and rescue the righteous (as in Ps 34:15–19). John's Gospel has Jesus declaring, "Very truly, I tell you, if you ask anything of the Father in my name, he will give it to you" (John 16:23). Scripture confirms that God does hear prayers and that God can intervene in human affairs: we read in the Bible that God splits the waters of the Red Sea so that the Israelites can pass over into the promised land, and that God stops the sun in the sky so that Joshua can triumph over his enemies.

The Gospel of Luke gives more attention to prayer than any of the other Gospels. Luke has Jesus telling two separate parables to illustrate that persistent and nagging prayers will be answered by God. After these parables, Jesus tells his listeners, "Ask, and it will be given you" (Luke 11:5–13), and concludes, "Will not God grant justice to his chosen ones who cry to him day and night?" (Luke 18:1–8). Luke notes that Jesus prayed regularly and routinely, especially spending time with God before facing opponents. Jesus's last prayer on the cross, however, is a prayer of acceptance rather than a pleading for help: "Father, into your hands I commend my spirit," after which Jesus "breathed his last" (Luke 23:46).

Throughout the Bible, though, we find many accounts of prayers apparently not being answered. God's chosen ones suffer exile, sickness, persecution, and captivity. Their prayers seem to be ignored. Psalm 22 thus begins,

> My God, my God, why have you forsaken me?
> Why are you so far from helping me…?
> O my God, I cry by day, but you do not answer;
> and by night, but find no rest.

At his crucifixion, Jesus repeats these words, "My God, my God, why have you forsaken me?" (Mark 15:34; Matt 27:46). This utter desolation is even more desperate than the prayer Jesus made three times prior to his arrest in the Garden of Gethsemane: "My Father, if it is possible, let this cup pass from me; yet not what I want but what you want" (Matt 26:39; see also 26:42, 44). Jesus warns his followers that they will have to endure suffering and take up their cross (Matt 16:24; Mark 8:34; Luke 9:23).

It seems that Scripture tells us two almost contradictory things: first, God promises to answer our prayers; and second, Christians will suffer, and they may sometimes feel abandoned by God.

These days I thank God for love and life, and I ask for help, patience, and guidance. I don't pray to win the lottery, and I find my prayers often answered. My own experience of life is that, despite times of suffering and feeling abandoned, great peace comes from being in a prayerful relationship with God and growing into God's way of seeing the world. This experience, however, will do little to comfort victims of violence and innocent refugees in their great suffering and loss.

The key question here is, "Can God intervene in special ways in answer to the prayers of the persecuted?" The idea that God might "intervene" to change the course of nature or work miracles is open to three critiques.

First, the idea of an interventionist God suggests that God is mainly "outside" nature, like an observer. As argued in earlier chapters, God is not in a "place" and God is not a physical agent. Rather, God is intimately present in nature as creation unfolds into its future.

Second, the need for intervention suggests that nature is on a determined mechanical pathway for which there is only one future, and that this future could only be changed through external intervention. This view of nature had some support from Newton's mechanistic laws of motion, but Newton's determinism has been replaced by the indeterminacy of quantum mechanics. Consequently, some scientist-theologians have argued that quantum mechanics and chaos theory allow for God to intervene in the world without the laws of nature being set aside.[1] As the theoretical physicist Brian Greene stated, "Matter has been dematerialized."[2]

Third, the interventionist theory entails a narrow view of God that fails to reflect on the significance of Creation and incarnation. God's Creation is an immense original intervention, and Creation includes the intervention of incarnation. Given these singular events, any further interventions are, as it were, par for the course. Even my unique being is a unique intervention on God's part. Developing my relationship with God, through thick and thin, helps me become more a part of God's life, God's will. As Richard Leonard concluded after writing *Why Bother Praying*, "Prayer is making space

---

1. See, e.g., the work of Francis Collins, leader of the human genome research institute, or John Polkinghorne, former professor of mathematical physics at Cambridge University.
2. Brian Greene, *The Elegant Universe* (New York: Vintage, 1999), 104.

for God to love us, for us to hear that and then, through the community of faith, to have the courage to return the compliment. It changes lives."[3]

God is constantly intervening in history, but God intervenes mostly through us. This is of little comfort, I know, for those who suffer chronic pain or who witness the terrible suffering of others. It is of little comfort for those who feel dryness in prayer. It does not help much to say that this suffering and dryness have always been part of Christian life. However, this great shared suffering and disappointment was profoundly experienced by Jesus's disciples on Holy Saturday, when they felt all was lost. Holy Saturday seems to represent a stage in life where we learn more about ourselves and more about God: we learn that we are small and vulnerable and know very little; we learn that we can love and support one another; and in the end, we can learn that God is love. We learn this especially through the intervention of the resurrection, but questions about Jesus and the resurrection are matters for another book.

---

3. Richard Leonard, *Why Bother Praying?* (Mahwah, NJ: Paulist Press, 2013). See also Richard Leonard, "Why Bother Praying?" online at www.thinkingfaith.org/articles/20130712_1.htm (accessed January 24, 2019).

17

DOES GOD LIKE BEING GOD?

"Do you think God likes being God?" What an insightful question! A thinking question and a caring question. The young person asking must already have the beginnings of a relationship with God, caring about God.

We constantly ask the people we care about—our family and friends—how they are doing. We ask, "How are you?" Can the same questions be relevant for God? Do we begin our prayer with, "Good morning God, how are you today? Do you like being God?"

Only God can answer this question. Is it just a projection of human concerns onto God's being? Could God be as self-preoccupied and self-centered as we often are?

We believe that God is personal, in the sense of being a "subject" rather than an "object," someone for whom loving relationships and feelings are important. For a Christian, God is never alone because God as a trinity of persons is always a community of ecstatic love. This oceanic concept of the Trinity, however, is impossible for our small human minds to fathom.

We also believe God is ecstatically in love with each one of us, and uniquely so. Sometimes we experience this love, especially when we feel the full richness of the gift of life and spirit. Christians believe that God is totally poured out in love, infinitely poured out in Jesus Christ. Emptied out. That's how much God loved the world.

In the Bible, we read about God's feelings. This is perhaps making God in our own image, but we read, for example, that God is well-pleased with Creation or intensely angry about the chosen people when they make sacrifices to idols. These stories are not about how God feels about being God, it should be noted, but about how God feels about us. Perhaps God is so totally concerned about us that it makes no sense to ask if God is concerned about being God.

We also read about Jesus's feelings. He weeps at the news of the death of his friend Lazarus and rejoices when his followers see Lazarus raised from the dead. He feels troubled in his agony in the Garden of Gethsemane and later feels despair and abandonment in his crucifixion. These are profound feelings rather than trivial emotions, and perhaps they reflect the feelings of the divine for the whole of humanity. Is Jesus's feeling of forsakenness about himself or about the whole of humanity and the entire creation?

To answer our questions, we need a deeper insight that allows God to be God and yet allows us to say something about God. For example, on the one hand, the Rabbis have a saying: "Do not answer questions for God"; and on the other hand, Emmanuel Levinas writes, "God...is bored to be alone."

Terry Veling provides a profound response. He suggests that "God is not overly concerned with God's own self....This is a question that rarely troubles God." The Scriptures are primarily about God's concerns, and they show that God is concerned about us, not about God's self. Veling writes,

> When Moses inquired into God's identity, God simply dismissed his question as somewhat pointless, as if to say: "Don't trouble yourself, I certainly don't." Yet we've been troubling ourselves ever since, not satisfied with God's lack of self-concern: "I am who I am" (Exodus 3:14), which means (among other things) that "I don't really worry too much about who I am. It doesn't really concern me too much. I am who I am." Moses learns that God is the one whose awareness is never a solipsistic self-awareness, but an awareness that is "well aware of their sufferings" (3:7).[1]

So, to the young person who asks, "Do you think that God likes being God?" we might reply,

> We can say very little about God, but perhaps we can say two things. First, God is very different from us. God's love is so great that God is totally unselfish and only cares about us. Second, I imagine that God loves us, loves the animals and trees, the stars, the whole of creation: God loves being. God loves everything that "is." God is so centered on us that God delights in us, feels for us, cares for us, and even suffers with us.

I imagine that God is infinitely happy being God, but just does not notice! This purity of being is God's holiness. God doesn't want our praise or worship or sacrifice so much as our being loving and just, delighting in creation, and bringing peace.

---

1. I thank Terry Veling for the insights expressed here. For the quotes from the Rabbis and Levinas, see Terry A. Veling, "A Theology of Religion: Reviving the Human Spirit," in *International Handbook of Practical Theology: A Transcultural and Transreligious Approach,* ed. Birgit Weyel, Wilhelm Gräb, Emmanuel Lartey and Cas Wepener (DeGryter, forthcoming).. On God's concerns, see Terry A. Veling, *Practical Theology: "On Earth as It Is in Heaven"* (New York: Orbis Books, 2005), 49ff.

WHERE TO FROM HERE?

After dinner one summer night, for no apparent reason, my cute and big-eyed six-year-old nephew went out onto the back deck, looked up at the darkening sky and called out, "God...God...." He waited a while, then shrugged his shoulders, looked down at his feet, quietly came back inside and got on with his usual routines. I don't know whether he knew we were watching him or not. He was beginning a journey of faith.

If you have come this far in this book, then you have completed another stage on this epic and unending journey to explore the mystery of God. Our pathway through these tricky questions has a deep history in Western thought, coming to prominence in St. Thomas Aquinas and his *quaestiones disputatae* (disputed questions) and later found in the beginnings of Isaac Newton's physics in his *quaestiones quaedam philosophicae* (some philosophical questions).

We have consistently used a traditional theological method to help answer the questions of the faithful today: exploring Scripture, tradition, Church teaching, the current situations of people, and the findings of contemporary theology, philosophy, and science. The point being made throughout this book is that *we can say something reasonable and intelligent about the mystery of God*. We can also explain why we can never fully comprehend God. I have asked you, fellow pilgrims in thought, to stretch your brains in three ways: first, to let go of narrow and simplistic ideas of God; second, to understand the reasonableness of our faith in God; and, third, to appreciate the ultimate incomprehensibility of God.

This is challenging work. We have taken some very small steps in response to our desire to understand God, but they have brought us to some clear and reasonable answers to our tricky questions:

> *God* is a pointing word: the word *God* does not capture the whole reality of God.

God is not made, rather God is: God is a being who is its own explanation.

The Bible's Creation stories are theological, not scientific: Creation is a work of love.

God is not an object out there in space and time, but an intimately present subject.

God is almighty in love, but love entails suffering.

God does have a plan for me, but I am free to choose the detail—and God stays close.

We cannot absolutely prove the existence of God, but belief in God is not unreasonable.

We experience God as a trinity of persons: transcendent, incarnate, and spirit.

There are traces of the one God in most religions.

God is intimately present in nature, but God is not the same as nature.

God hears our prayers, but we do not always get the answers we want.

While avoiding complicated theological terms throughout our journey, it may now be appropriate to introduce two terms from the tradition of the early Greek Church. When we have argued that we can say some reasonable things about God, we have been following what the Greeks called the *kataphatic* way. We can dare to say "positive" things about God, like "God is love." We need to be wary, however, of thinking we can ever fully comprehend God. For the Greeks, then, this *kataphatic* way would lead to the *apophatic* way. Strictly speaking, this meant that we could only say what God is not: God is not a piece of rock, God is not hate, and so on. In the end, the *apophatic* way points to the ineffability of God: we can say nothing about God. At this point, belief grows into mysticism, a personal union with God. As is often the case in theology and science, we need to hold these contrasting *kataphatic* and *apophatic* approaches together if we are to have as complete an understanding as possible of the reality we are exploring.

To say nothing about God is not the same as throwing up our hands in ignorance. To say nothing can also mean deep wisdom: there is a meaning, even if the meaning is not clear to us. A mystery, in Christian terms, is more than an unsolved puzzle. In Christian thought, the word *mystery* is a "sacred secret." We cannot work out the meaning of a sacred secret by ourselves because it is beyond our powers of comprehension. Nonetheless, the secret of the mystery can be revealed to us. We can learn something about its meaning by being invited into a deeper knowledge of God's view of reality. Thus, in the Gospels, we read of Jesus telling his disciples how fortunate they are because God has revealed to them the mysteries of the kingdom of heaven (see Matt 16:17, Luke 10:21–24). In using parables, Jesus reveals the mystery of the kingdom of God (see Mark 4:11, Matt 13:11, Luke 8:10). Similarly, St. Paul hopes that the Colossians will "have the knowledge of God's mystery, that is, Christ himself" (Col 2:2).

Philosophically and scientifically, we can know very little about God: we experience the possibility of God and the transcendence of God, but God remains a mystery. All we can do is wait for a word from God, like my nephew on the back deck.

But what if God were to choose to answer my nephew's call? What would be the most complete answer we could receive? Surely the most complete answer would be more than a voice from the sky, or an email, a tweet, or a vision in a dream. It would be a personal visit. In Christian faith, we believe that God truly comes among us in a fully human personal visit, so that Jesus is the Word of God, the fullness of God revealed to us, the answer to our prayer.

This coming of God in the incarnation raises an entirely new set of tricky questions about Jesus, but that is another step on the journey.

I wish each of you every blessing on the next steps on your journey of faith.